The Caring Trap

Jenny Pulling trained at the ~~Guildhall School of~~ Music and Drama, where she gained a teacher's diploma. She then turned to writing, and after working as feature writer on a local paper, she moved to *Woman's Own* in the same capacity. Since going freelance, her articles have been published widely in national magazines and newspapers, and her first book, *Feasting and Fasting*, was published by Fontana in 1985. She has also published short stories and serials, and devised and presented a number of programmes for local radio.

Her interest in caring was sparked off by her own experience of it, and she has since studied the subject and talked to numerous people in both the informal and formal caring fields. *The Caring Trap* is the result.

Jenny Pulling

The Caring Trap

A Fontana Original

First published by Fontana Paperbacks 1987

Set in Linotron Plantin
Made and printed in Great Britain by
William Collins Sons & Co. Ltd, Glasgow

To my mother and father, Elise and George - my source and my inspiration.

Contents

Acknowledgements

In the preparation and writing of this book I have been indebted to numerous people in both the formal and informal fields of caring.

Among them I should like to thank Adur District Council, Margaret Ball, Mary Blair, Stephanie Brierley, Paul Endersby, Queenie Ford, Peter Hudson, Joan, Helen Kahn, Phil Martin, Paulette Micklewood, Graham Millet, Judith Oliver, Rosemary Parsons, Anne Phillips, June Polden, Wendy Saunders, Mona Shaw, Edna Smith, Jenny Symons, Howard Thomas, Frances Walker, Avril Watts and Joan Welch. I am also grateful to my colleague journalists Iris Burton and Irene Morden who, through their publications, enabled me to reach many of Britain's 'forgotten army' and, last but not least, to the carers themselves, too numerous to mention by names, who entrusted me with their life stories.

My thanks, too, to Susan and Duncan who cared for me while I was writing this book.

Introduction

The death of my mother brought to an end a situation which had continued for several years: that of a single daughter caring for her elderly parent in a seaside town where it is all too easy to be isolated and lonely. The 'problem' had really existed for much, much longer, initiated by the death of her husband, my father, at a relatively early age – a bitter blow to our very united family.

Although my mother was a strong and stoical woman, she gradually became more reclusive, in spite of the efforts of both myself and my sister to give her life some purpose and meaning. During those earlier years, before the situation became acute, my sister married and I spent long periods abroad, which meant that we shared a 'part-time' caring role.

In the latter years, when my sister was occupied with two small children and things became increasingly difficult as my mother's health failed, it devolved onto me to become the 'carer'. We found then that outside support was hard to come by. With hindsight, we realize that this might have been due to a certain ignorance as to what was available but, to a greater extent, we discovered that any help on offer was measured in coffee spoons. The home help service was begrudged because I worked from home; the weekly visit of the district nurse to wash my mother was slashed to fortnightly and, although her greatest need was probably companionship, requests to an organization which specialized in the care of the elderly resulted merely in an infrequent telephone call.

Because of this lack of help, I experienced what I have identified in the many carers to whom I have spoken since: the dreadful burden of becoming almost her only daily contact, the claustrophobia, to the point of sometimes feeling suffocated, of living with the situation and, of course, the exhausting conflict of mixed emotions . . . the love, anger, frustration, and guilt!

My experiences must be at once unique and universal. In talking to carers, as well as many in the various caring professions, I have come to realize this. Every case has many aspects in common, and paradoxically each is a special, a 'one off' event. It is also one where, with all the available support in the world, the single carer is very much alone.

The situation in which parent and 'child' – or spouse and spouse – find themselves thrives, founders or coasts along, depending on events. Sometimes this has to do with the loss of the cared for person's faculties – physical, mental, or both – or personality changes which have altered them from the once familiar and beloved person they were. Nevertheless, and perhaps surprisingly, love has persisted, even if it is at times an exasperated love.

There are, however, two sides to the coin. Whether or not the situation of caring has succeeded or failed has not always depended on the sick or elderly person. Just as there are 'natural' parents and those who are not, so, I believe, there are individuals who seem born carers and, equally, those who are not. It depends to a certain extent on the carer's own sense of identity, urge for survival, or capacity for self-sacrifice. In my own case, I seemed to have come somewhere half-way between the two.

My life with my mother was not one of unmitigated harmony and it would be a mistake to pretend otherwise, although this is always a temptation after the event. The inevitable guilt experienced after a death and during be-reavement, the 'might have beens' and 'if onlys', encourage us to put the lost one on a pedestal and believe oneself, in retrospect, to have been totally selfish and uncaring. As one counsellor put it: 'We want to have been God: to have created a perfect and unselfish relationship, to have under-stood the other person completely.' No one human being can attain that and there are always faults on both sides.

If I am honest I know that we had our clashes; we were both less than perfect. But we were close, perhaps too close. As a family, we had always done everything together and my mother, I now know, lived in dread of being left alone. She became very possessive but, again with hindsight, I can understand her fear of being ill and solitary. I am now especially aware of the horrors of enforced solitude, as I have since experienced them myself. My mother was also a very remarkable lady with all her wits about her, a wonderful support to me in my work, with a warm and generous heart. We loved each other.

For my part, I feel that I was not the ideal person to look after her. I am not particularly domesticated, I need time to be me, and as a writer, I have a somewhat volatile nature. Above all, I happen to be unmarried and there was a rage inside me to live my own life, a sense, sometimes, that my time was running out. I was scarcely the creator of a serene atmosphere!

However, this was the role I had been allotted and I did my best to carry it out without losing my own identity and enjoyment of life as a still young woman, or sacrificing myself on the family altar. During my conversations with others in the same situation I found that they too shared these feelings. Some daughters seem able to give themselves wholeheartedly to the business of being a carer and I admire their apparent complete dedication. But within their ranks I have also met those in their late forties and early fifties who, having given 'the best years of their lives' to this caring role, are left with nothing and nobody, only the difficulty of picking up the pieces. This has sometimes embittered them and they have demanded 'Why me?' or 'Why me on my own?' It could have been so different if others had helped!

There were others who fought the situation from beginning to end, unwilling to assume the task and yet feeling it to be their duty, who made themselves ill until they stumbled on some kind of solution. This often involved turning their backs on formal assistance and paying dearly for the day and night help that was needed. Yet others, like the amazing P.M. of whom more later, have managed to bridge the gap between being an extremely loving and caring person during the parent's life, and then 'switching on' to a fulfilling if unconventional lifestyle after that parent's death.

With all this in mind, I thank the carer who sent me the following advice, after she had nursed her father for eight years: 'Accept the situation. Say to yourself: "This is my life as it has to be lived at the present time. I won't regard these as wasted years. I will get pleasure from any hours of freedom I have. What I am doing is worthwhile." When one accepts the situation,' she continued, 'one that can't be altered, then one is in control and there is no mental stress. It is when one fights against it that the trouble starts.'

Acceptance is all very well but there are times when anyone who is young in comparison with the person for whom they are caring rails against it; when the sense of injustice is overwhelming: 'Why me?'

There were many such times during the years I spent with my mother when I felt as if I were divided from the rest of the world by a sheet of glass. I seemed to see life going on beyond it, at one remove from myself – people enjoying themselves without a care, meeting, marrying, having children, just being together in a place from which I felt excluded. I seemed locked in a time warp from which there was no escape. It became very important to be able to talk about it but there were few people to whom I felt I could be honest without the fear of either boring them, or invoking their pity – neither of which I wanted. Those few who were prepared to listen must have found me self-centred, or so I thought.

I have seen a reflection of myself in the conversations I have had subsequently, with the women and men who answered my request for information in writing this book. The interviews – if you can call them such – were much more: an outpouring of dammed-up emotion. I became, simply, a receptacle for it; even though I might go armed with a list of questions, I rarely had to ask any of them.

Often, as we parted, they would say: 'I hope I've been of some help. I know it's certainly helped me just to talk about it to a stranger – get it off my chest. I have felt so alone!'

What I should like to say to them all is that they have been a tremendous help, encouragement and inspiration to me. If I allowed them to talk without censure or signs of boredom, then they have, equally, allowed me to eavesdrop on their most private thoughts and feelings, a privilege for which I am grateful. Often, after this initial outpouring, a dialogue has sprung up between us, the 'kinship' of shared experience which no one, unless they have gone through it themselves, can fully appreciate. And this has been invaluable, giving me an insight into how the situation might, or should, be coped with. Their views, both as past and present carers, have also given me a sense of the need to view the caring task as temporary rather than a life sentence. Of course, I say all this with hindsight. I know it would have been difficult for me to have thought this way at the time, but it is something of value, I feel, to pass on.

Taking care of an ageing parent until they die – seeing it through from the first hints of failing health to the imminent signs of mortality – does not allow for rehearsal and, as a rule, there is little or no opportunity for reference to what other people have done or are doing. There is need, I believe, of a counselling service. We are counselled in all the other periods of change in our lives; why not in this situation where, once you *have* taken it on, there is no reprieve, no divorce – it is literally 'until death us do part'.

The sense of isolation, of being the 'only person in the world who is doing it' is a *leitmotif* which came up again and again with the carers whom I interviewed. Why? Perhaps it has something to do with our British stiff upper lip – or as one professional carer suggested, the 'starving, behind-a-lace-curtain genteelness'. How many of the middle-aged women (and men, for that matter) who look brisk and busy, and appear to be coping magnificently, are bleeding to death inside?

A sense of duty was strong in many of the people I spoke

to. For example, I asked: 'Did you never think there might be alternatives to your assuming the entire responsibility? Dare I say it, did you ever think of putting your charge into a home?' But they had summoned up a memory of things past, of the caring mother, father or spouse of once upon a time, and now it just went against the grain to desert them. 'I would never forgive myself if she died in a home,' one carer told me. 'I nearly drove myself mad imagining her there just sitting all day while I was free to walk about. For my own peace of mind I had to fetch her home,' said another. Duty, in many cases, seemed an even stronger emotion than love.

There is also that aspect of society today, which Edna Smith, octogenarian founder member of the National Council for Carers and their Elderly Dependants, identified. We have lost the family as we know it. At one time, there would be large groups of relatives who probably never moved more than a few miles beyond the radius of the area where they were born. There would be a selection of daughters and daughters-in-law to step into the breach and take it in turns to care for the ageing parent. Edna Smith, speaking at the twenty-first birthday celebrations of the Council, looked to an apocalyptic future of bleakness where there would be fewer carers and a growing company of the lonely and old to be cared for.

It is fortunate, therefore, that this is offset by the increasing prominence of 'formal' as opposed to 'informal' carers. Something that surprised and delighted me while I was researching this book was the number of warm-hearted and devoted people concerned with improving the lot both of those who care and those who are cared for. There is Wendy Saunders, whose energetic organization of a temporary domiciliary scheme enables both parties to have a rest and holiday from one another. June Polden with her husband, Brian, have dedicated themselves to a group of those people who care for sufferers of dementia, in particular the disturbing Alzheimer's disease which claims its victims tragically early. Rosemary Parsons' concern for her little band of carers and the day centre she has organized for those they care for does not prevent her from being an efficient and compassionate organizer of the home help service; and Avril Watts' dedication to Age Concern has won her many admirers in the field. These and many, many more names which appear throughout the book are trying to redress the balance, and I have great confidence in them and in the future they are combining to create.

Meanwhile, our carers soldier on, too often with a sense of bitterness at having been pinned down in their role by the 'rest of the family', determined that their lives and freedom should not be impinged upon. And yet caring should not and cannot be looked upon as something that blocks our passage through life, but as part of a continuous cycle which begins when we are too young to care for ourselves. As one carer wrote to me: 'I would say to any person caring for the aged, give gladly and regard it as a privilege for we will all ourselves get old, one day.'

For those who have chosen to sidestep the issue, I hope this book may help them to understand and stop criticizing the limitations of those who are carers; and I hope it will encourage them to take on a part of the responsibility themselves in the future. I hope, too, that it will comfort those many, many daughters – because it is still more usually daughters not sons who take on the role – with the realization that however isolated they may feel, they are not alone; and their ranks can only increase with the current statistics of our ageing population. Have courage and re-member that what you are doing is worthwhile.

1. The Caring Situation

All through her life, Susie wore a ring on her engagement finger. If anyone asked her about it, she told them that it had been given to her by her lover when she was twenty years old. But her father insisted it was 'her duty' to stay at home and look after his wife and himself – to put all ideas of marriage out of her head. So her lover went away and his ring was her only reminder. She became the village spinster, running the post office for years until her parents died. At about that time her eldest sister was widowed and it was decided she should come home to be cared for by 'dear little Susie', who carried out 'her duty' for many years more. The death of this sister was the signal for another to announce that she would retire and return home. But at this point, Susie rebelled: she refused to take charge of yet another feeble and, this time, blind sister; she had had enough. A widower asked her to marry him and she accepted. There was no happy ending, however: her narrow upbringing meant that the physical side of matrimony was a trauma and for most of her short married life she was miserable.

This cautionary tale was told to me by an elderly lady who was herself born in the 1890s, when Victorian values still prevailed. At that time, there would probably have been about seventeen female relatives in a position to care for someone of over sixty-five; today, that number scarcely amounts to three. They were women like Edna Smith, who is now a lively over-eighty-year-old. She recalls a past when families were large and did not, as a rule, move very far away from the area in which they were born, when there was always a good deal of group support. Her own great-grandfather had ten sons and four daughters, her grandfather had eleven children. 'Even if they were married, they lived close by and were there to take turns when they were needed. Today families scatter. Marriages break up – children have various parents and step-parents and don't see why it is their "duty" to care for them. I looked after my father and my aunt, but there is no one to look after me.'

A rapidly growing demand and a shrinking source of supply in the cared for/caring ratio is a problem which is becoming ever more acute, particularly in certain parts of the country such as the south coast, which is somewhat unkindly called 'Costa Geriatrica'. In some of these coastal towns 25 per cent of the population is over the age of sixty, and that number is likely to grow considerably as age expectancy increases, alongside a diminishing group of carers, whether they be experts, social workers, professional carers, or the traditional 'daughters at home' like Susie.

Says Wendy Saunders: 'With all the good will in the world, when you get older you can't do the things you once did. You don't think about it when you're young. When you are middle-aged, you feel you ought to think about it but you put it off. We need to look ahead to get into the preventative bit before the crisis, but we don't, we think it won't happen to us.'

Growing older, however, has a changing image these days. No longer does a woman while still in her forties take to a shawl and bonnet like Mrs Bennett in Pride and Prejudice. We are seeing more sprightly and innovative 'oldsters' about. Our attitudes to what is 'old' are altering and, with a greater life expectancy, many people remain active and self-reliant much longer. They enjoy their independence and want to hang on to it for as long as possible. Edna Smith, an enthusiastic campaigner for education for the elderly, sees that a quite modest support is all that is needed to help such people manage. She feels there is need for discussion about ways and means which involve the whole community, the old and the young, and are not confined to the statutory bodies.

Sometimes all this activity can be mistaken in its direction, making for increased mobility when it might be a better idea to 'stay put'. Older members of the family, for instance, as they near retirement, may plan to move somewhere different, in the belief say, that it would be nice to spend their later years on the coast. As time goes by and one or other partner may die or become infirm, the other feels increasingly isolated, far away from the other relatives, and this in turn presents extra problems for caring.

Katherine, who is forty-eight and currently a 'part-time carer', is facing this dilemma with the knowledge that it can only become worse. 'Theirs is the old story,' she says. 'They moved down to Devon in their fifties, but it didn't turn out the way they planned. Nobody speaks to them, or if they do it's only on very formal terms. They can't find any real friends. My mother is quite all right, mentally, but my father seems to have retreated into another world. She is lonely and feels isolated. I try to encourage her by telling her she is coping wonderfully but I know they will need more and more care as time goes by.'

Distance exacerbates the problem of increasing dependence of one parent or the other, until it reaches the desperate stage where the 'child' is torn between parents and, if she is married, her adult home. One carer described a life of commuting between the two until the serious illness of her father forced her to 'abandon' her daughters in order to care for him. In spite of what is written and said about the disintegration of the family, familial bonds are not easily loosened and a whole range of emotions comes into play, such as guilt in the 'child' at not giving either parent or spouse enough time, and loss of pride in the parent in being forced to admit he or she cannot cope and needs help. This new dependence in those who have always had people dependant on them can create a lot of depression and anxiety, too.

During the past few years, a number of specialist groups have concerned themselves with the pre-retirement and retirement needs of elderly people. Several magazines have been created especially for them, to advise on various aspects of ageing and how to cope with it. While these may be admirable in some ways, professional carers like Avril Watts of Age Concern believe that it underlines the idea of 'them and us'. In her view, older people should be encouraged to remain within the community and not be set apart in a different place, as a different breed. People are people, she says, and for many of them retirement may have come a lot sooner than expected. It may be something of a shock and they are not ready to be relegated to the back seat yet. It would be commendable if general magazines ran such features so that everyone could read them and understand how it feels. After all, we shall all have to face old age one day. 'We are totally opposed to setting them apart as another generation,' says Avril Watts. 'They are part of us, a part of the community.'

Edna Smith agrees with this. She sees there is a need to establish that older adults are still adult, with experience, knowledge, ingenuity and adaptability that enable them to contribute considerably to the community. This 'belonging' she sees, too, as important, particularly in the context of the findings of her recent survey. This examined the care needs of those elderly people who had no prospective carers and showed that, at least for the next forty to fifty years, many older people will be living independently at home, in their local communities, for as long as possible and to a very advanced age. Most of these will either be living alone and looking after themselves, or living with a husband, wife, sisters, brothers or friends of their own generation, mutual carers, about half of whom will eventually become self-carers.

This may be no bad thing, according to another report. Studies have shown that, as a group, those living alone are healthier and more able to look after themselves than those living with other, younger family members. And if certain supportive services were available when needed to older people in their own homes, not just to those living in a home, this could boost morale and keep them healthy and self-reliant, enjoying rather than enduring independence. The same service could provide relief for younger family carers, especially those still at work. 'In the past, there were not these long-drawn-out deaths,' says Wendy Saunders. 'If an elderly person developed pneumonia it probably killed them.

Now there is therapy, drugs. Deaths are more likely to result from a degenerative disease such as cancer or heart problems. When people were crippled with arthritis some years ago, they ended up bed-ridden. Now, however awful they feel, it's "up and take your pill and keep on somehow." Obviously, this puts more responsibility on the people who are the carers and, indeed, increases the need for them.'

We become creaking doors – not ill but never really well – descending toward an unhealthy old age. Any carer who has had to cope with this decline will sympathize with Linda, who wrote to me: 'My mother came to live with us at the beginning of 1982 when it was no longer safe for her to cope on her own. As she became increasingly worse, I found the strain horrible and ended up being treated for mental illness.'

How often do we hear of seemingly vigorous elderly people who, within a year or two of their retirement, become apathetic and turn to their children, demanding their full attention? How important it is for carers to encourage those in their care to 'keep on keeping on'. As one home help commented: 'I know a couple who have their elderly father living with them and manage superbly, mainly because he is allowed to do things. He has his chores, such as walking the dog, which is invaluable to him in making friends, as he has moved away from his own area to a new one and pets are a great way of communicating with people. He also washes up, weeds the garden and does the dusting. The elderly have much to offer, but their main problem is boredom.'

The body inevitably slows down but, as many carers know, the elderly person who can be encouraged and stimulated to develop interests is less of a problem, both to himself and to others. The saddest sight is of those who don't do anything but sit all day, dwelling on the past. This used to be the image of many old peoples' homes but, fortunately, enlightened staff are now trying to break that mould. Some elderly people may have unfulfilled ambitions to education, as emerged in 'The Educational Needs of the Elderly', a report based on twenty-three interviews with retired people living in Edinburgh City Centre. Many of them wanted to be involved in educational projects, and expressed a desire for more stimulating provision. 'These retired people do not want to be receptacles for other people's knowledge,' ran the report. 'They have an awareness of the role they can play in contributing to this "fount of knowledge" because they have experienced more of life than most other groups in society.'

All too often society discourages this, according to educationalist Dianne Norton. In her view, it constantly undervalues the potential of retired people, and they themselves have come to accept this undervaluation.

Physical ageing is measurable, but the ageing of the mind is not as simple to calculate. It may possibly have more to do with external circumstances than we have realized. Growing older can be viewed negatively or positively, depending on the society into which we are born, its expectations, attitudes and traditions. It can become something of a vicious circle. If we begin to be less capable physically of performing certain tasks, those around us will come to expect less of us as thinking people; or they will lose patience, seeing that they could do the job in half the time. Then we dry up, becoming helpless and clinging. But if there is an anticipation of wisdom and status in the latter years, then we will respond, hold up our heads and not be afraid to voice our views.

In many societies the elderly person is the head of the household, referred and deferred to. When I lived in southern Italy I went into several households where granny ruled the roost. She might have been a tiny, wizened old lady but she always took her place at the head of the table when the family ate out on a Sunday. The Zapotecs of Mexico live an extension of the family unit, where every member of the family from the youngest to the oldest assumes some of the daily tasks. There is a sense of harmony, of 'rightness' to the pattern, which results in a sense of well-being. Everyone has that vital feeling that they are necessary.

Generally speaking, in almost every society or culture there are three quite distinct life stages: childhood, adulthood, and old age. Each has its season but in our modern society, something of this organic pattern is lost, changes taking place because it is 'time' and not because the individual is prepared for them. Sometimes, the prescribed transitions from one stage to the next seem inappropriate or arbitrary. For example, a youngster may marry when he or she is sixteen, provided the parents consent, but cannot vote until the age of eighteen.

People are forced to retire, whether they feel ready to give up the rhythm of their working life or not. Almost overnight, someone is transformed from a hale and hearty 'working person' into a being outside society, a 'senior citizen' who feels anything but, just because in the eyes of those who employ him he has arrived at the right age. Social welfare is doled out without the human touch and he is made to feel not that it is his due but that he should be grateful. He feels acted upon, his potency gone. Not only does this give him a sense of social redundancy but practical problems arise, too. When the income of a 'retired' household is dramatically decreased it often means that the increased leisure time cannot be balanced by funds to enjoy it. This reflects the low value society puts on the retired person's contribution, according to Heather McKenzie, former director of the National Council for Carers and Their Elderly Dependants.

In her book *Passages*, writer Gail Sheehy reviews the traditional, much more harmonious life stages which are described in the Hindu scriptures of India, 'each calling for a fresh response'. Student and then householder are succeeded by the age of retirement, when the individual begins his true education as an adult, and finally by the state of positive indifference, of bliss. In contrast, she remarks on the stages of a lifespan as it is viewed in our society today. She turns to the psychologist, Erik Erikson, one of the 'chartists' of these stages, although she changes his description of them from crises to 'passages' – each a turning point, each a crucial period of increased vulnerability. The passage to old age must be the most difficult of all, in the light of our current attitudes. We hear much about the mid-life crisis but not so much about that of elderly people as they feel they are being consigned to the scrap heap!

These attitudes can be infectious, and carers, too, may feel drowned in an atmosphere of helplessness. If the cared for feels that his or her activities have no meaning, are just a kind of occupational therapy – a way of getting through one day and into the next – the carer begins to feel that way herself. She may strive for a while to instil some enthusiasm, to create a stimulus, as my sister and I did with our mother. But when every pastime or idea is rejected, many carers give the whole thing up as a bad job and the couple coast along on this negative stream.

Incidentally, I refer to carers as 'she' throughout this book, which simply reflects the fact that more women than men undertake this role.

Two young men who worked among a group of elderly people in Switzerland probed into what these people considered to be meaningful or meaningless. Generally, they found the things that were done for others were considered full of meaning while those they did for themselves were without it. Many people thought back with longing to that time when they had their work and 'life meant something': the job laid down the rhythm of their lives. Suddenly there was leisure and the need to shape the day for themselves, to do what they liked. After a good deal of discussion, members of the group began to realize that selfishness need not be either bad or negative. But were they too set in their ways to be able to face up to the problem and resolve it?

The youthful Swiss encouraged their elderly colleagues to give the subject serious thought. They wanted them to try to explain why they had come to accept they were 'just made like that'. This lowered barriers which had prevented them from doing things they would like to do. And when they developed interests and activities they really wanted to pursue, this became a key to their happiness and fulfilment.

According to Dr Stephen Fulder in his book *An End to Ageing*, there is a need for a catalyst to turn social isolation from a curse into a blessing. Perhaps a part of that catalyst might come from the carers, for in helping the elderly towards realizing that they can allow themselves to be self-indulgent, this would, in turn, help them to discard some of the weight of responsibility of which they complain.

It might also be a good idea if professional carers took a fresh look at the way they approach the elderly. There is still a lot of room to improve communications between them, as the film *As One Door Opens*, produced by the Royal College of Nursing, showed. While the words spoken by a geriatrician were right: 'We want to encourage independence as long as possible but . . .', the message was undermined by a series of stereotypes which seemed to show there was still 'them and us'. To take one example: the geriatrician asked an elderly patient enough questions for her to show that she was fully in control of her faculties, then he looked across her to the Sister to ask if the patient had been sleeping well. The film showed elderly people doing occupational crafts, gardening, and having a jolly sing-song, but no one was shown trying to do anything new or challenging. Health visitors, discussing possibilities with elderly clients, referred to 'having' to cope alone. They made it sound as if doing things for yourself was just not a practical or desirable option once you were over a certain age.

Well-meaning as these professional carers are (they would probably be horrified to be told they created such an image), they could take a leaf out of the book of the staff who work in Danish sheltered housing. These are trained to be respectful and considerate towards the residents. It would be difficult to imagine them resorting to the over-familiar 'Gran', which is heard all too often in this country. Many elderly people reared on other mores and in full possession of their wits find it insulting.

Carer Angela said: 'Old people shouldn't be treated as if they are imbeciles. My mother wanted to know why the nurse kept on calling her "dear".'

Gemma, who is ninety-six, underlined this need to be treated as an adult, albeit an elderly one. She is thankful she has taught herself to type: 'You can't read all the time, even if you can see. Nor does everyone fall into the category of wanting to knit or sew. They want congenial company of their own kind with whom they can share experiences, past and present. They want to share in something, be involved in something.'

Without this 'something' and with an increasing sense of isolation from the situations which concern everyone else, elderly people become like Tom's mother. He is a 38-year-old postman with a wife and four children who is finding it very difficult to shoulder the responsibility of a parent who has now centred her life around him. 'Total dependence,' he says. 'The demand of exclusive devotion, a sly jealousy over any diversion that alters the work routine. Like many old ladies she utterly refuses to acccept a home help or, in fact, any outside agency. She demands just one, the acceptable one, who has to do everything.'

Joan's mother also turned her back on any outside help but in her case, Joan defined this as a fierce need for independence. 'Whether healthy or housebound, my mother disliked asking anyone to do anything for her. She was grateful to them for their help but felt herself to be a nuisance.' It is heart-rending for a carer to hear her charge announce that he or she is a 'nuisance', particularly because, with all the good intentions in the world, she knows there is an element of truth in it.

Like that beloved schoolmaster, Mr Chips, there are many men and women who strive to remain within society's circle; who, by sustaining their confidence in themselves, contribute valuable experience. Such a man is 91-year-old Ernest, who boasts he has never been out of work in his life. Even now, he 'works' at a morning 'pop-in parlour' serving coffee and snacks to the 'old people', many of whom are years younger than himself. Ernest's mind is razor sharp, his abiding hobby is whist. He lives with his son and daughter-in-law who are pensioners themselves, and usually goes on holiday with them to resorts such as Tenerife. But this time he had decided to stay home because he didn't want to miss his whist. 'When I first went to live with them, after my wife died, twenty-five years ago, I went to see the local doctor who wouldn't believe my age. "What do you put it down to?" he asked me. I said: "I don't smoke, don't drink and I've never been out with fast women."'

Then there was the case of the illiterate grandmother who was berated in a *Times Educational Supplement* article when she helped out at a local school. And yet here was a woman whom small children were not shy to read to. Perhaps for the first time in her life she had felt free to do what she wanted and she gave herself to it with gusto.

These two elderly people are living proof of the saying that it is never too late. They kept themselves adaptable to the changing circumstances in their lives and were protected against one of old age's greatest problems: isolation. Not every elderly person would want to accept such an undertaking, but there are numerous opportunities for them to become involved. Almost every town in this country has hobby and leisure associations and a local Age Concern office will have the information on those which are more suitable for the older person. Just as we all need warmth and food, we all need human contact – perhaps more so – and while carers may be deeply involved with their 'charges', they belong to a different generation and cannot always provide all the support that is needed.

Sometimes even the carer, who is possibly the closest contact, does not recognize the extent of this sense of isolation and loneliness. Many elderly people, for a variety of reasons, give a false impression of their feelings and, of course, as time goes by and the situation worsens, it becomes even more difficult to express them. Wendy Saunders spoke of the 'lace curtain syndrome' when all kinds of intense feelings of isolation may be hidden behind a calm exterior; when people feel, 'Yes, I am lonely. No, I haven't enough money – not to pay the bills, to keep warm, to join in. But I am too proud to say it.'

She feels that we have a special debt towards the people of that generation. 'The First World War took away many of their brothers and friends, the Second World War their husbands. We won't have to suffer such losses. And we have so many wonderful legacies from them – the right to free speech, the right to freedom – and yet how many people refuse to take any responsibility for them? If they see an elderly person wandering in the street, they telephone us, they tell us that "we" should do something about it. These people could join in the caring situation themselves in some small way.' Most of us are frightened of illness or disability, whether it be physical or mental, as Lord Windlesham wrote in an article some twelve years ago: 'Fear makes us afraid even of that which we could help most. So the community is content now, as it always has been, to shut its problem members out of sight. Give them a label, pay people to look after them, put our heads down, mind our own business and hope it'll go away.'

Often we blame the statutory bodies for not doing enough. Sometimes it seems as if red tape strangles any real help. But it is true, too, that the burden on both them and on voluntary bodies is becoming too much and they are working flat out to cope with the case-work on their books. Inevitably, the responsibility goes back to the door of the family.

Rosemary Parsons, home help organizer, sees her work sometimes as a juggling act, in trying to ensure that help is always provided when and where it is needed. Funding always helps oil the wheels but with government cuts the problem becomes more acute and, as Wendy Saunders admits, professional carers rely on the goodwill of daughters (and sons). 'We should be crippled without them.' The problem, she says, is that the situation happens to many people without their really taking in the implications. 'It may begin as a temporary situation. Mother loses father and comes to stay with her daughter. Time passes and she continues to stay, saying that in another week or two she will be able to cope alone. Almost imperceptibly, the situation is sealed into a permanent arrangement.'

As Katherine admitted: 'The idea of one or the other of my parents dying is a problem I don't want to face. It is our responsibility, my sister's and mine, but because she has children and I don't, I feel that the onus will be on me. I wouldn't think of putting my mother into a home. I think my

sister is more inclined to think that would be best but I don't
know whether I could do it.'

It seems there is need of a good counselling service to help
potential carers understand what their task will involve, to
understand the boundaries that must exist in such a relationship. 'The GP is not going to say "Have you thought
about what you are doing?"' says Wendy Saunders. 'Who do
you go to? There is counselling for the person who is getting
engaged or adopting a child. When it comes to a commitment
like this, you are facing a deteriorating situation. You will not
be able to get out of it. You need advice.'

Life, in Elizabeth's eyes, has never begun for her and she
feels bitter about all the time she has lost. She began to be a
carer when she was fourteen years old. There was no logical
discussion, no counselling. Suddenly, one day, she found
herself pitchforked into a situation which has continued until
the present day. Elizabeth wanted to share her experience
with me – that of caring for a parent, although her mother
was certainly not elderly.

When she had just turned thirteen, the family began to
suspect that there was something wrong with their mother.
'As the eldest of three children it was left to me to pull the
family through,' said Elizabeth. Her mother was taken into
hospital for tests and the young girl was left with the responsibility of taking five-year-old Susan to her first day at
infant school. 'It wasn't easy dragging a screaming child to
school and trying to explain why her mother was not with
her.' When Susan and twelve-year-old Keith were safely
delivered, Elizabeth had to rush a mile and a half to her own
school. At midday, however, she had to leave in order to head
back to collect the youngest child.

Her mother came out of hospital but did not improve. In
fact she worsened, becoming incontinent and, because the
local council refused permission for a toilet extension at the
back of the house, a commode and bedpan had to be brought
into regular use. To cap it all, Elizabeth's father, who had
always been a heavy drinker, took to the bottle again; he
could not come to terms with what was happening. On

Elizabeth's fifteenth birthday, a hospital specialist broke the news that her mother was suffering from multiple sclerosis. From that time onward, the teenager had to take over completely; there was no one to give her any support or help.

'To cut a very long story short,' she wrote to me, 'the social services more or less told us to "get on with it". For these seventeen years, I have done just that. I have devoted my life to caring for my mum, dad, brother and sister with virtually no help from anyone. I feel really bitter towards life sometimes, and I often wonder what it would have been like if only someone had said, all those years ago, "Let me help." But no one seemed to care and even today there are thousands of people who have to depend on family and, if they are lucky, friends, to help them. The whole structure of the health service, social work departments, and other so-called authorities is wrong.'

This theme of being forced to accept the responsibility even if they do not really want it is one that occurs over and over again in the comments of the carers to whom I have spoken. They may find themselves faced with a choice as to how they should play the role: they can either share the sense of isolation and hopelessness, or, if they manage to take a positive attitude, they can help those they are caring for to feel responsible for themselves, and respected.

Rosemary Parsons agreed that the task is not an easy one, and the problem is complex. 'Everyone has their individual breaking point. Some can take more than others and some can take different aspects to others. I find that doctors are usually too clinical: they see it simply as a medical problem and are not inclined to look at whether a person is *capable* of coping. I see more of that coping side, both in my work with home helps and in the carers' group we have recently formed.'

Angela has found GPs 'hopeless'. Her father was somewhat irresponsible and died in his fifties of a coronary without leaving a will. For the next thirty years she and her mother lived together, until the old lady died. 'The responsibility has put me under severe stress for the past ten years,' she said. 'As long as they think there is a carer, they won't help. It is just piling the pressures on to one person, which is madness.' Nevertheless, she had an innate sense of duty and said that she would have cared for her mother, whatever the circumstances. 'A lot of women are like that. We haven't learned to be ruthless.'

The situation was almost the opposite for Caroline, who was bombarded by people advising her to think more about herself. A local coordinator of rest homes was very helpful, and at one time Caroline's mother entered one of them with the idea of allowing Caroline to live her own life. But even as her mother left her, Caroline knew it was not what she really wanted, and experienced 'mental torment'. 'I couldn't enjoy anything, thinking of my mother in there while I saw other old ladies out, shopping, sitting in places having tea. One night I was up until dawn, agonizing, and it suddenly came to me: "Who has the ultimate responsibility? I have, and I can do something about it."'

She compared this with another crisis in her life, the time when her marriage was called off and she felt powerless to do anything about it. But this time: 'I thought, "If I spend my last penny, I don't care". I knew that I should have such a burden of guilt if I didn't bring her home. I am paying back the debt I owe. I am caring for the mother she once was.'

The situation and how the roles are cast has many variations, but there are familiar circumstances, too. Often a mother and daughter end up together because of the earlier mortality of men. Olivia and her mother faced the deaths of father, husband and fiancé within a matter of weeks. They closed ranks, Olivia staying on at home instead of moving to the house where she and her husband-to-be had planned to live. It seemed to Olivia that doctors and hospitals deliberately gave the impression that things were worse than they were, in order to hand over the responsibility to a caring relative. But it is not only doctors and hospitals which appear to have deserted them. Many of the carers with whom I discussed this longed to be able to explain to outsiders the 'turmoil and frustration' that an octogenarian can bring into their lives. They long for a little human contact which would not only normalize their own lives but bring some colour into those of the people for whom they care. Dorothy's friends 'disappeared' when her mother had a slight seizure and her and her husband's lives became 'lonely and uneventful'. 'We would willingly entertain at home, and we did, before Mum's illness, but though she still retains her faculties and would dearly love company, we find that so-called neighbours and friends avoid us like the plague.'

Neighbourhood support would make the lot of the carer and her dependant much easier to cope with. The focus of attention of the elderly person would be dispersed instead of, as is so often the case, all his or her irritability and frustration being centred on the sole carer.

In order to show her carers and helpers what it is like to be handicapped and vulnerable, Rosemary Parsons conducted an interesting experiment. She ran courses where they were blindfolded or one of their limbs was tied up, and asked her students to note the resulting feelings, the anger and frustration. It was a help in understanding why some of their elderly charges can be so aggressive.

James, whose wife is suffering from cancer, understands these emotions and encourages visitors. 'My wife gets bored with one person, and I am there all the time. After friends or family have been she's bright as a button, a different person.'

If statutory help is not readily available and neighbours lead their own lives, you would still imagine the family would rally round. But here again, the carer often feels she has little or no back-up. It begins to seem to her as if she has been 'elected' by the others. In a subtle but determined way, many brothers and sisters appear to have decided upon the one who shall shoulder the responsibility, and marvellous excuses are found to ensure that they will not have to step into the breach – financial reasons, family reasons, distance . . . Tony, trying to analyze his feelings towards this sense of being forced to take total responsibility, said that the over- whelming feeling was not one of anger towards those who could share but would not, not even a sense of burden, but one of weighty responsibility: 'the need for daily phone calls and curtailing outings in order to keep in touch. Eventually, the strain manifests itself in physical signs, if only in exhaustion or sheer tension.'

Many of these 'children' are too proud to ask for help and give the impression of coping well, which serves to lull the conscience of the rest of the family. Avril Watts sees many examples of this in the course of her work at Age Concern. It may come as a surprise to many when the caring system breaks down, as it did in the case of Sarah, who ended up with a nervous breakdown. Unless you have experienced the situation personally, it is often hard to appreciate just what goes on behind the doors, and some bystanders may comment that the carer has 'brought it on herself by being on the spot all the time'.

Olivia is aware that there are several who think that way about her. 'It is true that I was there,' she says, 'but it wasn't my choice and surely a woman must be allowed a life of her own while living with a parent. I am fifty years old, the only child of my 85-year-old mother, and I can honestly say that for the last twenty-odd years my life has been dictated almost entirely by what has happened to her.' Olivia adds that this feeling is exacerbated by the attitudes of neighbours and friends – or so-called friends. She feels she has become nothing but a shadow or echo: 'the daughter'. 'The constant greeting every day is "how's Mother?", even if they don't know her.'

Caroline recalls visiting her father's mother when she was a child. She remembers the closed-up smell of the sickroom and the two daughters who cared for the old woman. She never believed she would be in the same position. 'I get so fed up with the comments people make, their insinuations that there is something wrong with me and my relationship with my mother. It's just been laid on my shoulders. I have a brother who is very fond of her but my sister-in-law has a subtle way of alienating him from me.' There is some truth in the saying that a son is a son 'til he takes a wife, a daughter's a daughter all her life.

It seems you cannot even generalize about loyalty between sisters. Nancy's sister, Ruth, has been 'wonderful' taking it in turns to sit with their mother while Nancy shops or gets her hair done. Grace's attitude is quite different. She is determined she will not become involved in her sister, Delia's, role of carer. She remains obstinately on the outside. Delia has dropped hints, telephoned with problems, finally come out with it: would Grace please share the burden, having mother to stay at weekends or during the week? But her sister retorts with every suggestion under the sun from day centres to meals on wheels, never offers to help her by shouldering at least some of the responsibility.

'It's the single woman who gets stuck with it,' said Joan Welch, local secretary of the National Council for Carers and their Elderly Dependants. 'I was lucky, my brother was very helpful. He did everything he could to help.'

Although, as Avril Watts commented, many of these women care for their parents with 'enormous joy', as time passes there is the inevitable glance back over the shoulder to the things that have been lost. By the time many parents have died, their children will be in their late forties and early fifties, past child-bearing age and with a decreasing chance of getting married.

One of my most memorable experiences during the writing of this book was my conversations with P.M., bubbly and full of life, whose philosophy is inspiring and stimulating. She told me that she did not regret not getting married, although she understood that her mother had hoped she wouldn't. At eighteen she met a man who was very much older than herself; the match was quashed by her parents. She smiled and shrugged and said: 'One thing I would love is to be cherished by someone. I don't regret not having had children, either. I wanted to be a Norland nurse but Mamma said: "I am not having my daughter washing other people's babies' nappies."'

Elizabeth is much less reconciled to a life which has turned out to be very different from the one she dreamed of at the age of thirteen. 'My sister is engaged, my brother is married and never comes to visit. I will be thirty-one in a couple of months, still unmarried. I don't even have a steady boyfriend. During those long seventeen years and even today I am trapped. There seems to be nowhere to turn and no one to turn to. The question has to be asked: "Who cares for the carers?"'

2. Living Together

Often, of course, a good relationship continues between those two people who are living under the same roof, sharing their days – and nights – together. But sometimes it can be difficult. There may be resentment on one or both sides: that the frail or infirm need to ask someone to do things for them, that the other must give up certain aspects of their lives. And yet, and in spite of all these hazards, there are many thousands of people who embark on a true labour of love – there are some one and a quarter million informal carers in Britain today, according to the Equal Opportunities Commission. Thousands have been caring for ten years or more and one in two becomes mentally ill as a result of the strain.

These days we hear a great deal about our 'uncaring society' and how we have such little regard for the elderly and infirm, but I think it is time to put things into perspective. One of the most powerful messages that has come across to me from the people I have spoken to and the many letters I have received is of the depth of caring of many towards other members of their family – to the extent that they sacrifice a large part of their lives, or at very least their energies and tranquillity. They are people like Stephanie and her brother, both married, both with children, who told me that their parents' plight 'fills their lives'. They and many others, both formal and informal carers, have moved heaven and earth to allow those people for whom they are caring to stay where they want to be.

Caring and coping – that is, dealing with the situation successfully from both points of view – can be two very different things. It seems clear to me that if carers are to cope and, therefore, to help those for whom they are caring to cope better with their problems themselves, it is important that the weight of their task is lightened wherever and whenever possible. Unfortunately, the fate of many of those who have contacted me is to have been broken by the burden or left, after the death of their charges, feeling incapable of living a life of their own, their purpose and autonomy gone. The arrival of a grandmother into the family home, which might, in happier circumstances, have lent a new dimension, has all too often seemed like the advent of a cuckoo in the nest; the former loving relationship between a mother and daughter has been destroyed by the classic clash of two adult women sharing a kitchen and getting under each other's feet.

Part of the problem is that boundaries are not recognized, as Wendy Saunders has put it. There is a need to point out: 'This is my life: half yours but half mine, too.' If that cannot be said and adhered to then situations will continue to arise such as the quite shocking one of a husband and wife who felt they never had any privacy in their own house because her mother lived with them. When they wanted to talk, they would go for a drive and sit in their car.

Age Concern's Avril Watts believes that families should stick together and a theme of the association's work is to aid them to do so in order that the elderly people can remain integrated in the community. 'But there is need for a couple to have time alone and there should be an understanding that they must have privacy, no matter how much the elderly person requires care.'

Living together is not easy. Many marriages take a long time to 'settle', as the couple gradually becomes used to each other's idiosyncrasies. Imagine how much more difficult it is when, as in the case of several couples known to Age Concern, the wife has agreed to her husband's parents coming to live with them. In one case, when the younger man died, the widow was left to care for her two elderly in-laws. I believe I should find that an almost intolerable situation and I think many people would agree with me. How tempting to say: 'They're not related to me by blood; how much loyalty do I owe to my husband's elderly or disabled parents when he is no longer with me?'

I shall write about Mabel at some length because she seems to me such a remarkable person, one of a vanishing breed. Faced with this situation, she has stoically carried on, treating her role as carer with professionalism, and yet I know from speaking to her that she is a person with deep emotions who would dearly have wished life to be otherwise.

Mabel's husband, Bill, had parents who lived in the north, and about nine years ago the telephone calls began: Bill's mother was becoming increasingly frail and had had several falls. Whenever this happened, her son would drop everything and drive the 250 miles to satisfy himself she was all right. Later, it was arranged that the elderly couple should come south for a holiday. The milder climate, they all agreed, would do them good. But, as Mabel said, once they were installed she had a premonition they would never go back. 'We started off on the wrong footing,' she said with the hindsight many carers develop. 'When they first came, we should have been firm and told them we would be taking breaks together and that they would be left alone. But we didn't, and that was the beginning of the end for us.'

Eight years passed. At first the elderly people lived *en famille* but Bill decided to make them their own sitting-room in order to allow himself and Mabel more privacy. Then tragedy came. Admitted to hospital, Bill was diagnosed to be suffering from cancer and within a year he was dead. Mabel returned to the home which she had shared with her husband and sons, to take charge of her parents-in-law. I think it says a lot for her courage and character that it never entered her mind to make other arrangements for them. Her quiet strength is chastening.

From the time she wakes at seven, her day is centred around the 'old people'. She gives them breakfast and does their rooms, which includes emptying the commode, before she begins her chores. The couple like their main meal in the middle of the day. Mabel's eyes were on the clock as she spoke to me – they were, she said, 'sticklers for meal times'. 'And I never leave them for any length of time. They worry.'

Her one 'freedom' is her car and she is pleased that she continued with her driving lessons after her husband's death. Sometimes she goes out in it in the afternoons; evenings can drag, but her lowest ebb, as many people find, is Sunday. Mabel keeps herself busy, going to church and then doing all her housework. 'I don't like to put upon people at weekends; they have their families.'

A friend of mine wisely said that we should never 'underestimate the strength of an elderly couple'. Mabel smiles when she hears the 'old people' argue but she knows that it is their continued companionship which keeps them going. Her attitude towards them is ambivalent. While she says she would never dream of separating them, which might happen should they go into a home, she has dreadful stabs of the sense of injustice about it all: that at ninety-three and ninety-four respectively, they have each other while she lost her husband.

Mabel might be called a 'born carer', according to Joan Welch. There are some people capable of accepting the role, others who definitely are not.

The National Council for Carers and their Elderly Dependants, as the name suggests, is intended to support carers, both single and married, as well as those they are living with and caring for. It has been responsible for many improvements in the situation, including a study of the legislation affecting their problems, and promotes policies that can improve their lot. Edna Smith, who was involved at its inception, has described how its concepts have changed as the role of carers and, indeed, of women has changed. The Council was actually founded by a Methodist minister, Mary Webster, who, although a sick woman herself, cared for two infirm parents. At that time, Mary's hours were flexible and she was able to devote the necessary time to them: but she began to ask herself how other women fared, whose lives were perhaps more conditioned by time than hers.

Says Edna Smith: 'At that time, it was usually women who did the caring. She, Mary Webster, saw that those who did care had to do a lot more for a lot less money. So her first focus was for equal opportunities. If the family was living in a council house, for example, and it belonged to the parents, the carer could be thrown out when the elderly people died and not allowed to continue the tenancy. We asked Members of Parliament, "Who looked after *your* mother?" when we were campaigning to alter this. The reply was somewhat shamefaced: "My sister!"' The Council has moved with the times and now helps all carers, men and women. 'The more you help one the more you help the others.'

Caring is international. I received one letter from two sisters from the Netherlands, both in full-time jobs, who live with and look after their octogenarian parents. Their own days of retirement are not far away and they both 'dread it'. 'Three women in one kitchen,' wrote Hilda, 'will be two too many people.'

In the day in, day out, year in, year out situation of living with someone else it is often not the major things which annoy but so-called domestic trivia. This is particularly hard to cope with where there are two adult women, each with her own way of doing household jobs. I know this from my own experience. When I look back to that time I find it almost absurd, and indeed sad, that arguments should have erupted over the way one cooked, or even washed up – but that is how it is. In the claustrophobic atmosphere where the world of many elderly people has shrunk to just four walls (and sometimes this applies to the carer, too) everything is magnified. I have not come across this situation to the same degree with a parent-and-son relationship, although here there can be other clashes and problems. One carer remarked to me that she found it difficult to cope with a situation where 'one moment you are in charge, and the next pushed back into the child's role again. My mother is very strong-minded; let's be frank – bossy. She won't yield an inch to me on how to run things.'

Her comment and many others, in letters I have read, sound familiar. Although, as I have said already, every caring experience is unique, in some ways I find I can nod, smile or shake my head ruefully as I recognize a feeling, an idea, and this is one of them. But with hindsight, I can understand it very well. The kitchen is the last stronghold, the place where many women of my mother's generation ruled supreme. It is a hard thing to relinquish.

Rosemary's house is, fortunately, nothing like ours was. I shuddered as she described it to me: a dirty cluttered-up mess of things she would like to throw away. 'Old plastic buckets full of washing in soak, dirty knitted washcloths, smelling. Tin bowls full of rotting apples, bits of wool, buttons and bits of rug . . . all the sorts of things I know she has a perfect right to but are hard to live with if you have dreamed of a neat little bungalow of your own.'

How I could identify with Rosemary and her sense of being swallowed up. How I longed, as she does now, for that place of my own and now that I have it, how lonely it seems sometimes! Nothing lasts for ever. But at this moment, Rosemary's yearning is acute: 'Just somewhere,' she pleads, 'somewhere I can be an adult woman.' Her resignation reminds me of the heroine of Mary Gordon's wonderful novel *Final Payments* who, living and caring for an invalid father, describes the family home as a place of 'life having accumulated before you were old enough to fight it'.

'Fight' is an extraordinarily apt word. In many of these stories which carers have done me the honour of relating, there is the idea of a battle for power. I have admitted the antagonism which sometimes existed between myself and my mother, when the situation became too much for us both, even though we loved each other very much. Many of my friends who are single daughters tell me of the conflict of emotions they experience, whether living with their mothers or seeing them often – or rarely. 'Of course we had rows,' Angela confirmed to me yet again when I discussed this feeling with her. 'We took it out on each other. Basically we loved each other but we had flaming rows because I wanted to lead my own life.'

Although generally these days someone lives with another person and takes care of them because they want to, there are still many instances where that does not apply. 'In the old days,' said Father D., an Anglican priest, 'Grandma was looked after by the family even if they didn't want to look after her and it often broke the family up, so that she was shipped about from brother to sister. She was loathed, sometimes, but they couldn't do anything about it.'

Even today there are cases where, even though the parent has emotionally or even physically abused a son or daughter in earlier life, that 'child' assumes the caring role later on, as a duty. More often, however, the couple have decided to live together, after a lot of thought and discussion, if not actual choice. Although it is a very emotive situation, I think it is important to try to be objective: to realize that elderly people should be helped and encouraged, wherever possible, to deal with their own lives; and that those who take on the responsibility for their care may lose the quality of their own lives. I write with hindsight, of course, and I understand very well how feelings can override commonsense when you are in the middle of it all.

One of the worst motives must be for a carer to 'take on' someone because they worry about what other people might think if they don't. Far better that alternatives be looked into, and alternatives there often are! Edna Smith points out that since she cared for her mother, the structure of our society has altered and continues to do so. The elderly cannot assume any more that when they reach that time of their lives when they need help to look after themselves, they will simply sell up house and move in with younger members of the family. The pattern of marriage has altered – there are more divorces, more single parents, and families which are the product of several marriages. The old 'insurance' for old age is gone.

Any would-be carer needs to give the matter deep consideration. If she is married and unless that relationship is strong and without problems, an extra person could be the 'straw that breaks the camel's back'. If she is single, she will have to be aware that unless she makes a real effort to preserve her social life and independence, she is in danger of losing both.

The problem of making the 'right' decision between moving elderly parents or helping them to stay put is one close to Margaret Ball's heart. As director of one of the 'Staying Put' scheme's centres, she is very aware of the conflicts. Her own mother and father are mutual carers and, in spite of her disabilities, her mother is able to carry on cooking, thanks to alterations which have been made to the kitchen and the house generally. There are handles everywhere, including on the stairs, which allows her to keep active.

'There is a case for encouraging them to stay in their own home,' said Margaret, 'so do consider the alternatives to their selling it and moving in with you. I know that if I had my mother living with us, she would need someone always with her. I would rather help my parents to stay where they are. They retain their independence and dignity and I think that is important. As it is, my mother can tell me off when I visit her and I can storm out of the door.'

One problem, she said, is posed by the picture elderly people may have of 'family life', and how nice it would be if everyone were together. They often become disillusioned. Margaret and her husband had planned for his father to move in with them. During the six months it took to prepare his bed-sitting-room, she tried to explain that life would not be a question of their spending all their time together. While she would cook his meals and give him a home, she had her own interests to pursue. But the elderly man could never quite accept this; in his mind, he always believed it would be different.

Moving out of one's home in later life can be a traumatic experience, but sometimes it seems to be the only solution. P.M. had had her mother staying with her 'on and off' for years, but after the death of her father in 1977 mother and daughter decided to sell up the London house and move to the coast. P.M., who is a wonderfully unconventional person, fell in love with her small flat there, principally because of its panoramic view over the sea. Light flooded into the room where I met her, almost a year after her mother died. 'The problem was it was over a shop,' she smiled, 'and Mamma said that one didn't live over a shop. She hated it.'

When Caroline's forthcoming marriage was cancelled she decided to buy a house in both her own and her mother's names. Gradually, it has become hers as she takes over the authoritative role. 'When you are young and have problems, you go home to mother; before you can turn round, the roles are reversed,' she says. Nevertheless, she counts as one of her blessings the fact that she has a secure roof over her head.

In spite of the problems which both have faced, which they have resolved or time has solved for them, P.M. and Caroline, in comparison with many of the other carers I spoke with, are not badly off. P.M. missed the independence and stimulation her work gave her, and her lifestyle changed as her mother's need of her grew. Caroline managed to afford to pay for help by continuing to work although she, too, finds it difficult to have much of a social life. But both have come through with their identities intact. This was not the case for Helen, who has ended up feeling bitter about the burden that was put on her. Early on, she was faced with the problem of living under two roofs, dividing herself between her father's home and living with her two teenage daughters whom she had brought up virtually alone. To add to this, she was also trying to carry on the family business.

At first, the arrangement was one she managed to cope with: she would visit her father once a week, stay overnight and do his cleaning and shopping, then return to her own home. But the situation became more complicated when her father developed an illness and then she stayed with him three or four days at a time, spending the rest of the week with her girls. When it was confirmed that her father had cancer she realized she could no longer leave him alone, especially as she had a semi-invalid brother living with him who could not bathe, shave or dress himself. The horror of the duties she had to perform until her father died haunt Helen still, and the conflict between those two homes was a nightmare. 'I've lost my own home and the business,' she said, 'and since my father died, I have had to fight the authorities to be able to stay and take care of my brother in the home he has lived in for the past sixteen years.'

Relationships are complex things. There is probably no such thing as total unselfishness. We all need to feel necessary, we give love in the hope of receiving it in return, and in the case of a carer, it may well be that the needs of the elderly-to-be-cared-for may be used as an excuse for not facing up to other aspects of life. There are times when the 'self-sacrificing' carer is, in fact, escaping from work or social situations which she dislikes or cannot deal with. In mediaeval times, such a woman would 'get her to a nunnery'.

Judith Oliver feels that this can be a female weakness. Such carers may become too intense, over-possessive, excluding their dependants from any other contacts. 'We turn them into self-centred tyrants. If you fussed that way over a child, people would say you were spoiling him.'

In this context, she thinks men are 'better' carers. They regard the task as an extension of work: calculating how many hours they can put in, making arrangements for what they cannot cope with. They even use similar terminology for the two situations. 'One engineeer caring for a severely disabled wife told me that it had "tested his marriage to destruction",' she said. 'Another one-time soldier devised an intricate method of booby traps and barricades so that he could detect when his senile wife got out of bed in the night.'

Some women carers continue to juggle job with caring. Angela remembers 'never carrying a handbag, always a shopper' when she looks back to the days of working while caring for her mother. She never relaxed for a moment, she said, but used to be late for work in the mornings because she shopped on the way, and even so spent her lunch break shopping, too. 'As long as I brought in the grub, my mother managed to get her own meal. She had hers in the middle of the day and I had mine when I got in. We did try the meals on wheels service but found it useless. Old people need their vegetables and orange juice. Their appetites must be stimulated.'

While Margaret coped with a large house and garden for seven years, she carried on a full-time and hectic secretarial job until she decided to ease up and retire, six months early, in order to spend more time with her elderly father. 'My life had been one mad rush for so long.'

Caroline's trusty Moped proved a tremendous boon to her because it meant she could get home at lunchtime from the schools where she was doing supply teaching. She didn't want to give up her work and preferred to pay a series of four women to 'granny-sit'. 'If I gave up my job I might as well say "goodnight",' she told me. 'I know myself; I couldn't just stay at home and look after Mother.'

'I've been a shop assistant, a waitress, a holiday camp chalet cleaner. I used to have a good clerical job but I had to leave it and from then on have worked part-time with the jobs going lower and lower down the scale,' said Olivia. 'Now I work the permitted hours a week in a secondhand clothes shop. If I earn any more, my benefit will be stopped.'

There are no set hours for someone who takes on the 'job' of caring. It can be a round-the-clock task, every day of the year, involving every conceivable duty from cooking to nursing, charring to toileting; often, if he or she has given up work to be a stay-at-home carer, there will be little money on which to manage, possibly sparse outside assistance and no status. Any form of financial help such as the Attendance Allowance, Mobility Allowance, Severe Disablement Allowance and Supplementary Benefit are paid to those who receive the care. It is up to them to choose whether or not they will hand all or part of it over to the person who is caring for them.

Until recently the Invalid Care Allowance, paid to people

who are not working but are caring for a severely disabled person, was withheld from women who were married or living with a man. But in March 1985 a married woman, Mrs Jacqueline Drake, was awarded this allowance by an appeal tribunal, on the basis of an EEC Directive of December 1984, which stated that there must be equal opportunities to claim social security benefits and that discrimination on the grounds either of sex or of marital status should end. The DHSS appealed against the tribunal decision and the case was taken to the European Court of Justice, where Mrs Drake won her award. Despite this victory Judith Oliver, director of the Association of Carers, has been distressed by the threatened suicides of two of her members, who were not able to benefit because they did not satisfy all the conditions involved in the claim. The award now stands at £23.25 a week.

While it is true that many of the carers with whom I spoke received the Attendance Allowance, again it seems to come about after some effort rather than automatically. Caroline was not at home when the assessor/doctor called and she told a wry tale of how they almost missed the allowance: 'Mother was in such good spirits that day, dressed and really believing she was capable of taking care of herself. She told the doctor she was able to go to the shops. 'I don't need my daughter,' she told him, 'I can cook and go to the library.'

Financial worries crop up time and time again in the stories of carers. There are all kinds of extra expenses in such a situation: special food for different diets can cost a lot more; extra warmth, not to mention a few luxuries, would make life much easier to cope with. It seems to be a short-sighted policy not to support better people who are doing such a good job in keeping their elderly dependants out of a home or hospital.

According to Pat Young, former editor of *Geriatric Medicine*, the Danes are streets ahead of us in their attitudes towards caring for the elderly. When she visited that country she was impressed by the enthusiasm and humanity of the various officials she met. The basic pension for a single person is approximately £250 a month, tax free, and there is no earnings rule which would prevent someone supplementing this as much as they wished. In addition to the basic pension, writes Ms Young in an article 'Denmark – Utopia for the Old' (*New Age*, Spring 1985) they can receive financial help, for medicines, spectacles, special diet foods, hearing aids, foot care, other physical treatments, dental treatment and dentures. Medical care is entirely free and there are special grants for heating and housing costs. A Danish pensioner can afford to feed and clothe himself well. He expects and receives a good standard of living and there is a pension office in his locality which he can telephone and call in at, if he needs advice.

As the elderly person becomes more frail, there is plenty of home help, nursing at home, day centres and meals on wheels – in fact, the full range of services that are provided in Britain but on a bigger and better scale. As in Denmark, our government has a policy of community care, the aim being to help elderly people to stay in their homes as long as possible, but in Britain the money does not seem to be available to provide it. Night nurses do not reach everyone and there are problems with home helps, especially at holiday periods. The home helps in Denmark, on the other hand, offer their clients a full caring service which begins when they are woken in the morning and ends when they go to bed at night.

There may be an attempt to try to recognize the plight of the carer in Britain, but for many of them the wheels are turning far too slowly. They need that help now; for some, tomorrow may literally be too late, for they have reached the end of their tether. I remember the call I had from an elderly woman who has cared for several relatives during her life, including two invalid husbands. Her second has now arrived at an acute stage of his illness, in need of constant supervision, and she has developed an anxiety state. Irene could not face the thought of her husband coming home after a short stay in hospital. She was fortunate in finding an understanding director of one of the state homes who was prepared to take her husband in for a while and give her extra respite.

And it often appears that the help provided is not right, in the circumstances. Mabel, following the suggestion of a health visitor that she needed a home help, found the woman 'very brusque' and decided to cope on her own. She is very independent, does not like to ask for help and keeps her home spick and span – but at what expense to her own physical and mental health! Angela remarked that the home help who was allotted to her was 'useless'. She would concentrate on one job, for example, clean the windows – and 'upset the window cleaner and make another mess. Mum was in pain and couldn't take it. In the end, I did everything.'

When P.M. developed arthritis and found it difficult to use her hands, she was given a home help. But government cuts made it possible for her to come only once a week so P.M. ended up paying for extra help. Once again, this compares unfavourably with the Danish experience where the home help service is attached to the nursing service, the two working closely together and operating from the same base, under the direction of the same person, a senior nurse. This avoids the divisions of responsibility which exist here.

In sharp contrast to this was a chilling report I had from one Scottish carer. She asked the social services for help for her mother when she wanted to take her son up to university. 'I was told: "That had better be the truth as I am not paying out for a home help if you are sitting across the road." Now they all say that because of the stress I was under at the time, I misunderstood. But I feel that in return for being a caring daughter I have now been branded a neurotic liar who imagines conversations.'

Like any service which involves human beings the home help service cannot be 100 per cent perfect. There could not be a more caring person than Rosemary Parsons, the home help organizer. Rosemary is always determined to get help where it is needed and she has no time for those organizers who say that such things are impossible. 'If there is a need that need will be met,' says Rosemary. 'It doesn't matter what it is – in a crisis I get the help to them even if I have to juggle with the hours, afterwards.'

During the time I was with my mother, we had several home helps who ranged from the mediocre, via the willing ladies who carried out their duties to the letter and no more, to an exceptional home help, Louise, a dear friend to us both. Louise is a German woman, married to an Englishman – a kind, sensitive person who identified with every one of her 'old people' even though some of them were obviously ungrateful, even downright unpleasant. There were many days when the weather was bitter and other, less dedicated, helpers might have rung in to say they could not get into town. Louise managed it, somehow, putting chains on her boots, literally, when the roads became slippery as glass. She would also return to some of her charges after her official working hours if they were ill because, as she told me, she 'drove her husband mad because she couldn't sleep worrying about them'. To my mother she was gentle and kind, one of the few people who bothered to sit and talk to her. I have nothing but praise for Louise and it was a sad day for us and her other charges when she decided to take early retirement. She had worn herself out being too good.

'Home helps, at their best, will do anything,' says Rosemary, 'certainly not just housework. Sometimes other things are much more important. They may get someone ready to go to a day centre, or give a carer time to go and have her hair done, or feed the dog or budgie . . . the idea is to enable the person in question to stay in his or her own home.'

Rosemary's home helps are an example of an excellent, self-motivated team, who band together at Christmas time to fund-raise for the dinners which are distributed then. According to Mary Blair of the Money Advice Case Work Bureau, people have very stereotyped ideas of the home help, but she is often an important intermediary. While the elderly person may not mind too much if the place is dirty, he or she will welcome the stimulation of the home help to start a conversation and have a cup of tea. Mary described various aspects of case-work, such as the confused elderly person who loses her pension book or, having collected her pension, doesn't know where she has put it. Then there is the lady who has got herself into serious trouble because she can no longer cope with the electricity and water rate bills. A home help may come across demands tucked away in odd places, or the 'disappearing pension money' and report it to her supervisor so that wheels can be put in motion to solve the problem.

One very successful story of this kind of liaison began when an elderly woman who was suffering from cancer decided to sort out her affairs; in particular, what would happen to her husband after she died. Said Mary: 'I saw this lady, asked the necessary questions and it was arranged that the money should be managed by a London solicitor, while we coordinated the practical side of things here. Now I see the widower weekly, and try to coincide with the timetable of the home help, who is now the carer in this situation. She can tell me the practical issues that arise; she sees that he has his sandwiches or his meals on wheels and gives him his 'pocket money'. If he were to handle all his pension, he would probably spend it in a pub. At the same time, he enjoys her coming to the house because she was their home help when his wife was alive and they can share her memory. Honestly, he wouldn't know what to do without her.'

When Rosemary Parsons interviews to recruit home helps, she looks for someone who cares, rather than a superwoman. She will need to prepare them for such eventualities as being accused of stealing, or having to deal with incontinence. It is not, as might at first appear, an easy way to earn money as a part-time job.

Although Angela and other carers turned their backs on the home help system, it is important for both carer and cared-for not to try to exist under the same roof in isolation, but to try to bring others onto the caring scene from the onset of the relationship. Just as the elderly or infirm need this outside friendship, so do the carers. If they feel that their physical and mental health will suffer, they must try to take preventative steps. This is a particular danger in the case of a single daughter. Many women give up the chance of marriage or other relationships with men because they enter into such an intense relationship with their dependent parent, putting his or her needs first as their most pressing priority. 'In truth, a carer who marries should still be able to give loving care to an elder,' says Heather McKenzie. That way she is less alone and can call on the support of her husband and, later, children.

Several carers have told me that their parents were set against their having outside relationships and they understood why: the fear of being left alone, deserted. But, as Ms McKenzie advises, this interference should be anticipated and guarded against. She points out that the parent has had a fulfilled life and the adult child should bear that in mind, as well as the fact that she won't have her parent for ever. Various carers I have met faced this sort of 'blackmail' and dealt with it with varying degrees of success. Caroline said that after her abortive marriage plans, she found that the first years living with her mother were not too onerous, as the elderly woman was quite mobile and she was able to go out and entertain people at home. 'She was never the kind of mother to interfere,' she said. 'At one time I could even go away for a few days but since 1975 my activities have been increasingly curtailed. You lose impetus, too. One thing I find hard is to mix in society with married women who have children. Their major concern seems to be should they go to Crete or Greece for their holiday? Put new covers on the settee? I am weighed down with these colossal cares. It is years since I was taken out. Oh, the luxury of having a man about the house!'

Phillipa said that she had been determined to ensure that when she was left on her own she would not exist in a vacuum. But, 'It really does take an almighty effort to keep up with friends and interests when there is so much to be attended to.'

Perhaps the most chilling story was that told to me by Laura, who reached the point of feeling so lonely and isolated living with her mother in the family home that she signed on with a marriage bureau. She had to do it secretly, as she was certain such a move would cause arguments. Not long afterwards she met a pleasant man who lived close by. 'Although we were not attracted to each other enough to fall in love, we liked each other enough to have been good friends and a bit of company.' But her mother objected and disliked the man 'for silly reasons', creating a bad atmosphere on the infrequent occasions when the couple met.

'The last time – just an afternoon and evening in the country – when we returned home at nine in the evening I found that my mother had decided to clean the outside windows.' This was something she never did, as a rule. Consequently, the couple arrived to find a reproachful neighbour installed, ready to tell Laura what she thought of her, out enjoying herself with 'men' while her poor mother had fallen off the steps and lain in the garden, helpless.

Laura realized that her mother would continue going to such desperate lengths to make sure she bound her daughter to her, and that unless she was willing to risk the elderly woman really injuring herself, it was to be an end to her days out. 'I gradually dropped the boyfriend,' she said, 'who wasn't too keen on the situation anyway, and resigned myself to being "just the daughter" again. I know it was emotional blackmail, but how can you call the bluff of a mother of eighty-plus?'

It seems clear that however difficult it is, anyone who takes on a caring role must remain, or even become, a little aggressive for their own sake. They should not allow their lives to become so overwhelmed by the demands of another person – no one has the right to expect all of you. But situations like Laura's are insidious and creep up on you. I have also noticed that many of the women who become carers are people who put the wishes and needs of other people before their own. For several reasons – upbringing, conditioning, their need to be seen as 'caring' by the rest of the world – they cannot bring themselves to say 'No, on this occasion I am going to please myself', or 'Yes, today I am going to treat myself to something I want, do something I wish to do.' But this attitude should be developed as part of an essential survival kit.

In my own case, I tried my best to be caring and to sustain some kind of routine in the home that would reassure my mother that there was someone around who was concerned with and for her. But I also went out with friends and away on holidays; at times I was perhaps too aggressively determined to maintain my own identity. Nevertheless, as another carer said to me, 'I don't think I was any the less a good carer just because I was hard, sometimes.'

It is important, too, to look into all sources of help both from voluntary and statutory sectors so that you can get some respite and have time to be yourself. There are several options for this short-term respite. It is possible to arrange for the elderly or disabled to go to a day centre once or twice a week, but there may be the problem of transport if the carer cannot take her charge there herself. Another problem is persuading some stubborn elderly people to go! In my mother's case, she had an image of bingo-playing grannies and flatly refused. Another idea is a short stay in a residential home. The cost will depend on your income: if this is below £3,000, it may be about £28.50 a week; if your income is more then it could amount to between £100 and £200. If the doctor prescribes it, it is also possible to obtain nursing care at home, as in the case of P.M., whose nights had become so disturbed she was suffering ill effects herself, and eventually obtained a five-night service every week. As for night sedation: 'Who do you sedate?' joked Wendy Saunders 'yourself or her?' The home help service gives other relief and there are private agencies who can supply granny-sitters. Some of the carers to whom I spoke took matters into their own hands, advertised for and paid for the necessary relief.

For the past four years, Wendy Saunders has been

involved with a family hospitality scheme and during that time she has helped about 250 elderly people. Her work is centred around developing and placing on a register families who are prepared to offer short-term care of the sort they might give to their own elderly relative. It gives the elderly or infirm person a holiday two or three times a year, and allows the carer the opportunity of a break, too. The hosts are paid £66 a week but this is stressed to be of secondary importance. If the guest can afford it, he or she pays the whole fee or part of it. In some cases, the DHSS will oblige. Wendy said that it is a specialist task to find suitable homes and to match guests and hosts. When she interviews her families, she makes no bones about what they should expect.

'It is not dear old Miss Marple sitting in the corner, knitting and giving out pearls of wisdom,' she said. 'These people are frail, physically, maybe depressed. They need a holiday. They may require a commode at night, they may become confused when they are tired.'

She talks to the elderly potential visitor, too, to make sure he or she understands the arrangement. Over time, she has learned to weigh up families and visitors and can usually judge whether one person would fit in with the Smiths and not with the Browns. But there are problems, both in finding sufficient people who will open their homes to someone who needs this respite, but also in contacting the sort of people who would benefit from the scheme. The problem in the south is the discretion and genteelness of people who would like to be hosted, which makes them reluctant to come forward and express that need. 'They don't like the idea of being grilled by a social worker,' said Wendy. 'They're afraid to come into my office, believing they are going to be put under the microscope.'

She is wry about the strange attitudes of some elderly women who may be well into their nineties, and beautifully cared for by daughters in their seventies. 'The mother will tell me, "I'm all right. I don't need a holiday. My daughter cooks me beautiful meals, she's a wonderful carer." But I point out something these ladies don't realize – that their daughters are elderly, too. They may have been retired for ten years. "Like you, they are getting older," I tell them, "and they are having to look after two people."'

Although the caring role may endure twenty-four hours, day and night, Wendy sometimes finds that it is not only the elderly person who, reliant on her carer, becomes possessive, refusing any outside intervention. Sometimes it is the carer who finds it hard to let go her charge, or admit that she is not the only person who can cope. She will feel hurt if her mother comes home, singing the praises of her host family. One woman who had devotedly cared for her mother for many years was always being told that whenever the elderly woman visited her other daughter, she always had a wonderful time. When she died, she left all her money to the other, favoured daughter.

'When people go on holiday or are with someone for just a few hours the whole situation is quite different,' says Wendy, 'No one can expect that intensive kind of caring 365 days a year, at home. But it is valuable to give these people short breaks, relieving the relatives who are caring for them and enabling them to stay at home much longer.' It would certainly relieve people like Joan, who has constant arguments with her mother in the evenings when she comes home from work, tired and wanting to be quiet, while her mother has been alone all day and wants to talk.

'Hostile communication is better than no communication', according to Helen Kahn, another caring lady who runs a branch of the Council for Voluntary Services. One of its schemes is neighbourhood care which develops a network of people who live in the vicinity and who are prepared to keep an eye on the elderly and infirm, again with the object of helping them stay in their own homes. Another project involves volunteers who help out on a more casual basis than the statutory home helps – they will collect a pension, or do some gardening. The volunteers are not paid and are often gaining experience in the field in order to work within the social services. But this informality can be an asset to many of the elderly, who are too proud to accept formal help. 'There are a lot of people who reject "the welfare",' said Helen. 'They view their privacy as a divine right. They have probably been people who helped others in their time and don't like to be on the receiving end.'

Pat Goose, whose bureau runs a 'pop-in parlour' where elderly people can come for a coffee and a chat, agrees that this aggression is a positive thing. 'They are reacting and it shows they are keeping on. They come here and argue over their seats, they fight over the secondhand clothes, even who will get the top slice of toast with the most butter. This is so much better than the withdrawn elderly person who stays at home and gives in. Isolation can bring on depression and become a vicious circle.'

Day centres, according to Pat Gosse, are not all 'tea and bingo'; there are many with all kinds of other facilities such as crafts programmes and drop-in lunch facilities. The big problem is transport; although people like members of the Red Cross are very helpful, it is still sometimes difficult to get elderly people to the centre they want to attend. Looking to the future, she sees an increase in the problem as the ageing population grows, but she does not believe that this should be echoed by an increase in residential nursing and rest homes. There is a real need for integration. 'We need to have more day centres, to increase the home help service, and to improve means of transport – we need more money.'

In the final analysis, according to Heather McKenzie, the success of the carer in coping with the problems of caring will depend on her awareness of what to expect, her ability to make decisions and adhere to them and her knowledge of what help is available and the measures she can implement to help her lighten her burden.

I cannot endorse this attitude more. However difficult it is, it is important for the carer not to become swamped in caring for another person. The result might resemble Laura's sad situation: 'Mum and I could have been the dearest of friends and I could have helped her just as much if we hadn't lived together all the time. I have insomnia and am so depressed I feel I can hardly speak or drag myself around. At times I scream the place down and have to avoid the neighbours for days afterwards. I throw things at my mother or try to strangle myself.'

Said Lydia: 'We are the women who are neither married nor on our own, single in a society which thinks of people in couples. If you are a carer, no one cares a damn.'

3. Under the Same Roof

There are now more than eight million people over the age of sixty-five in Great Britain and their percentage in our population is still growing. It follows that we have an increasingly urgent need to understand just what arriving at this age means, in all its aspects – physical, psychological and social – and to provide health education both for those who care and those who are cared for. Unless we do, our health service will crack under the burden of coping with the largest ageing population in the history of the world.

On a more personal level, I have shared with many of the carers to whom I have spoken a sense of incomprehension in the face of dealing with someone who is growing older. I know that if I had understood more clearly the processes involved, I might not have been as impatient as I sometimes was. I know, too, that many of the cared for do not understand what is going on, and develop anxieties and phobias which could be helped, if not solved.

For all that they are so close to their charges, carers are among the guilty in taking it for granted that the elderly know instinctively how they should behave, when often in fact they are bewildered by all the changes going on in their bodies, their minds and their lives with the passing years. Elderly people are 'expected' not to be very active, they are 'expected' to lose their memories. Such seeds of anticipation breed fear. But age does not necessarily mean bad health or loss of abilities, and there is no body of evidence to suggest that intelligence declines as time goes by. Sometimes the capacity to remember more recent happenings may diminish, but some octogenarians are perfectly able to absorb and retain new information if it is relevant and interests them.

Inevitably, though, changes come about – bones break more easily, skin wrinkles as the tissues thin out and lose their elasticity, hair colour fades and the posture becomes less upright, while the dry weight of the brain shrinks from about 1,300 to 1,000 grams. Ultimately, it is not the changes in themselves which shape old age but the way in which we view the process of ageing. If, as in some cultures, happiness is based on youth and movement, then the old may feel they are without significance. But if old age is seen as a time of consolidation and reflection, these physical changes do not seem so important. I believe that we could all do with some education in the ageing process.

It might be a good idea if old age was a topic included for discussion in school curricula, as was recommended at the conference of the Vienna International Plan of Action on Ageing. A greater knowledge of the subject could positively change the attitudes to ageing in our present generations. It was also suggested that the mass media might be used as a means of promoting the participation of the aged in social, cultural and educational activities within the community and that they, in turn, should be involved in formulating and designing those activities. As Edna Smith points out, this would reinforce the notion that they are still responsible adults. 'Because people have reached the age where they are not "allowed" to work, it doesn't mean to say they are not still adults; that, suddenly, they are no longer acceptable; that they should be dead and not a problem!'

But people often behave in the way they are expected to behave. I have watched elderly people playing up to the image they think others have of them. One carer told me how her parents appear entirely different when they are with outsiders. 'With me, they are helpless. They are never well. By that, I mean that however healthy they may be at the time, if I ask them sympathetically they can always come up with something that is not quite right. It is my fault to a certain extent. I am forever anxious and together we seem to generate this anxiety about their health. I never see them as ordinary people; they are always "my parents" and I worry about them.'

But people are people and whatever their age, they

intrinsically remain the same. And yet, almost from childhood, we have stereotyped images of the 'elderly'. In youngsters' books, there is the plump and cuddly granny who bakes scones and wears a shawl – that is, if she isn't a wizened old crone. The media's approach is often similar, full of condescending remarks about 'old folks' or 'senior citizens'. Newspapers splash headlines about an elderly lady who stands up to a mugger, an old man who gains an Open University degree, as if these were miracles. On television and radio, the same attitude prevails: a stereotyped view with no special attempt to portray them as the people they were and often still are.

Has the media created this image or does it merely reflect our own concepts? Age Concern carried out a survey among the elderly housebound to find out how they felt about the way they were shown on television. Most of them had reservations, believing that elderly people usually face adversity with much more humour and are generally tougher than they are seen to be. A powerful assumption is that all people as they grow older show physical and psychological disabilities, are not able to function autonomously and lose their role in society. For example, a home help wrote to me to describe one of her client's households, where the family had taken over the care of elderly parents who were not ill and were still capable of doing things for themselves: the old couple felt 'taken over' and, left with nothing to do all day, they just imagined complaints. It is a wrong and negative conclusion that old age equals helplessness and if carers are to help elderly people and, in doing so, help themselves so that they may remain fulfilled and healthy, both physically and mentally, we need a far more age-integrated society.

Says Joan Lestor, MP for Eton and Slough: 'It is very depressing to visit homes for old people and realize that so many of those running the homes make assumptions about what old people want, and that so many of these assumptions are wrong. They presume an intellectual void, that old people don't read, and want only light entertainment and crafts – their intellectual backgrounds are seldom taken on board by their carers. There are certainly some changes beginning but many old people still dread going into an institution, not because it is an institution but because they are afraid that their special interests will not be catered for.'

It was to provide options other than moving the elderly or infirm into such homes that the Anchor Housing Trust 'Staying Put' concept was born. The Trust had been worried by the little it could do to help applicants, the majority of whom needed sheltered housing which was not always available to them. Their idea was to 'unlock help' which would enable these people who were finding it difficult to manage without help to continue to live in their present homes in comfort and convenience, yet preserve that precious independence. The 'Staying Put' scheme offers money, skilled advice and practical guidance through the complexities of building finance and building work, to those retired people whose homes are in need of maintenance and repair, or require adaptation to match their changing needs.

Margaret Ball, who heads one of the centres of the 'Staying Put' scheme – there are seven throughout the country – described the dilemma of some people who, as they grow older, want to stay put in their homes but are being faced by increasing problems. The kitchen may have become difficult to use because they can no longer reach the cupboards; health problems such as incontinence mean numerous and exhausting journeys upstairs because there are no downstairs facilities. There will almost certainly be an increased need for warmth in our cold climate, one that is not properly met by open fires; another growing anxiety may be the garden, which has become too much to cope with.

'Once we have been able to sort out problems, often starting off with an informal home interview, they are happy to stay put. But sometimes when we see people we find that what they really want to do is move. They may not come out with it at first; they are afraid to make decisions about themselves, and sit tight.' When Margaret Ball realizes that this is what they want, she probes gently about neighbours, and may discover that there is someone who does a bit of shopping for them, someone who takes the washing off their hands – and so on. 'If you have caring neighbours like these, it is probably better to stay where you are.'

Because many elderly people may have lived in the same house for years, they have ceased to 'see' the need for repair or maintenance. Often it is a son or daughter who consults the 'Staying Put' team for advice or help. Or it may be that the carer who is living with her parent is herself elderly, and not able to do what once she did. According to Judith Oliver of the Association of Carers, there are more households in Britain containing adults of several generations, the most frail being cared for by people who are themselves elderly, than ones containing a child. 'Staying Put' will advise on the one condition that the owner of the property is a retired person.

Just as bounding good health gives a person an outward-going attitude to life and the ability to keep up with friends and activities, conversely, worsening health breeds despondency and negative attitudes. The ageing person begins to feel that if he (or she) is not expected to stretch himself, there is little point in doing anything but slouching in an armchair, and the vicious circle is completed when this apathy creates ill health. One of the goals of carers must be to try to help the elderly sustain their interests and build on their vitality so as to avoid that downward spiral; and this is no easy task, as I know well. A pattern of thinking may have been formed that it is difficult, if not impossible, to break through. When those you care for have arrived at a certain age they are, to a great extent, conditioned by habits and attitudes from the past. It is hard to introduce new ways of eating, to urge a regime which incorporates relaxation and exercise. Either they cannot discipline themselves to follow it, or they simply don't want to be bothered. It reminds me of an incident when, after social workers had done everything they could to persuade a group of elderly people to go on an afternoon's outing, the response was 'Why can't they leave us alone?'

A friend of mine encountered the same reaction when he thought he was doing well by volunteering to spend several evenings a week with the elderly in a state-run home. His ideas of brightening their time were dashed when he realized that what they really wanted to do was watch television. Even while he was attempting to talk to them he could see their eyes slewing round to the small screen. Probably, he concluded, they would blame him for making them miss an episode of their favourite soap opera. Nevertheless, I believe that it is necessary to persevere in the hope that somehow you will get through.

Improving physical health is most important, too, and here I am chary of the role of the average GP. He is all right if your charge develops an infection, or falls and breaks a leg. But if your goal is to build longer-term vitality and resistance to infections, then I suggest you leave him out of your calculations. If I am honest, I must say I have found many GPs to be unhelpful. A typical reaction is to scribble out yet another prescription to add to the cocktail of drugs, and when depression or anxiety inevitably show themselves, to add to the collection a tranquillizer. If the carer becomes anxious, he may suggest she take a tranquillizer, too! But I am not indicting all general practitioners. I was cheered by a conversation I had with a young woman doctor who was very aware of what needs to be done but felt frustrated at the lack of time she had to talk to her elderly patients. Disillusioned, she had turned to community work.

Our medical system seems to be designed to stave off death a little longer but with scant thought of improving the quality of that lengthened existence. It often admits its own limitations: while infectious diseases have largely been combated, degenerative illnesses are more stubborn; they take time to develop and by then are difficult to treat. Some people will argue that the average lifespan has increased dramatically over the century because of modern medicine. But research shows that a good deal of that increase has rather resulted from improvements in public hygiene; those longer lives are not necessarily healthier or happier. One survey showed that the degree of disability suffered in the latter part of old age has increased. The older we get, the more likely we are to become frail and incapable of doing things for ourselves. Another survey pointed out that 200,000 people in this country have trouble making a cup of tea unaided. All this puts a greater strain on their carers.

General practitioner Dr K. takes a rather pessimistic view of ageing, believing that our genetic make-up plays a major role in how we arrive at old age. But he does add that taking a reasonable amount of exercise, eating well but not too heavily, should offer a better chance of health in old age. He sees a large part of his work with elderly people as 'keeping them ticking over and as comfortable as possible. I don't see why, for example, you should submit them to unpleasant investigations if you can only resort to palliative measures, if anything is discovered. It is a decision doctors are often faced with: whether to, or not; when to, and not. You assess each on its merits.' In his view, it is hard to dictate a health plan when you are coping with an organism which is running down, anyway. 'Take the man who has been smoking all his life. If you stop him smoking, it is not going to make much difference. So let him keep his cigarettes and have his chest infections.'

Curative medicine's approach is the drastic dose when the damage is done. By the time we feel bad enough to go to our doctor, the symptoms show that the health problem is advanced. Then treatment will deal with those symptoms but does not really alleviate the cause of the disease itself. Ideally, our later years should see us following a course of action which has begun when we were much younger. This would involve preventative measures which had taken into account the individual, his strong and weak points, his particular body make-up and lifestyle – for often the problems of old age are a result of the habits and experience of a lifetime.

However, from my own experience I would say it is never too late to do something. I echo Peter Hudson, homoeopath and clinical nutritionist, who is currently developing a life extension and rejuvenation regime. According to him we can, to some extent, reverse the biological ageing process, improve the mobility and agility of body and mind, rebuild flagging tissues and organs and recapture the energy of younger years. In his book *Why Die Young?* he writes: 'Scientists studying the question of ageing for the past few years have found that there are two basic processes. One is the ageing pattern but the second is dictated by the way we live and how much we allow our bodies to be abused. Add to this the very real dangers of early retirement when the mind and body change down several degrees, together with the possibility of a lazier lifestyle and the process is accelerated again.'

At one time, I was very concerned about the numerous bottles and jars of drugs which had appeared on my mother's medicine shelf and decided to seek advice. I consulted practitioners of what is now called 'complementary' rather than 'alternative' medicine, and on their advice began to give my mother several natural preparations including evening primrose oil. There is no doubt in my mind that we managed to reduce her high blood pressure by the use of this oil. Our GP often expressed surprise when he took a reading, and would say he 'didn't know what she was doing but that it was doing the trick'. I did not enlighten him as I had already experienced his views on alternative medicine.

Avril Watts shares with me a concern about the over-prescription of drugs. She told an amusing but hair-raising story of two old ladies who had lined up their various bottles of tablets and, comparing them, were actually competing with each other as to who took the most. Indeed, experiments in a London teaching hospital have confirmed the remark of one geriatrician who said that some of the most dramatic effects of drug therapy in the elderly are achieved not in the initiation but in the withdrawal of treatment. During trials, patients had all drugs, except those necessary for survival, withdrawn, and the improvement was such that many were able to return home.

'Gently does it' should be the maxim, however, when it comes to considering changes in an elderly person's diet, activities or the drugs he or she is taking. My mother was most cooperative when I suggested we added or subtracted things from her eating plan, although I could never persuade her to eat more vegetables.

It is not easy to convince your charge that it might be better, in the long run, not to take so many tablets, because you are coping with fear and anxiety about illness. Often it is the elderly patient asking for short-term but swift relief from a complaint which prompts the prescription of drugs, as much as the doctor's initiative in providing them – then both are locked in a conspiracy, unwilling to give up the medication even though the side effects may be insidious and unpleasant. Drug treatment, as Dr Stephen Fulder has said, becomes 'a juggling operation between the benefit and the harm'.

Unlike holistic medicine which seeks to treat the person as a whole, to try to bring that body back into balance and health in its truest sense, many drugs treat symptoms only, and merely mask continuing ill health. It takes patience to go for a longer-term regime which includes changes in eating habits and lifestyle, too. It is also important to balance this approach with a commonsense attitude to orthodox medicine. An elderly person may need drugs to keep his or her blood pressure stable. To stop suddenly taking them could be fatal. But where the carer believes medication is superfluous, she can talk to her doctor, asking him if he can withdraw it gradually, and at the same time taking him into her confidence as to the alternative measures and advice she is taking for the health problem in question.

Peter Hudson was a great support and help during my mother's latter years. He gave me a lot of useful advice. It was he who suggested an excellent preparation which contains slippery elm food and which is helpful to anyone suffering the pains of diverticular disease. We were not so successful with the high-fibre diet prescribed by a hospital, but between us we worked out a diet which kept her on a more or less even keel. Peter Hudson's book is based on dietetic principles and I found it helpful. 'Irrefutable evidence suggests that many thousands of people are suffering from drug-induced diseases,' he writes. 'In many cases, these are far worse than the actual symptoms the drugs are prescribed for. Of course, not everyone will achieve the age of one hundred but at least middle age need no longer be that time of life when we think we will begin to feel better in time.'

As we get older, sleeping patterns change: we may sleep more or we may sleep less. For those who are bothered by the problem of waking in the small hours of the morning, unable to get back to sleep, it might be comforting to know that this is not real insomnia but a part of the ageing process. One can be aware of the physical effects of age on appearance and faculties, but our sleep process also ages in a less apparent way. Many elderly people believe they 'ought' to sleep their eight hours, right through the night, and ask for sleeping tablets. Generally speaking, however, daytime catnaps can be deducted from the total daily sleep needs. Such naps can add up to two hours a day, leaving only a further four or five hours to be taken at night. It is also a good idea to take a short nap around mid-evening, rather than to feel sleepy and decide to go to bed around ten. Around three or four in the morning the elderly person may awaken, and although he or she will then have had his full sleep quota he may worry that he has not had enough, and perhaps get out of bed. The alteration in blood pressure can sometimes make him unsteady on his legs, and this is an occasion when falls occur.

For one reason or other, elderly people may resort to sleeping tablets. The problem here is that several of their beneficial effects are illusory. Apart from disrupting dreaming sleep, which is very important to us, most are designed to help you to get off to sleep, and keep you asleep without too much disturbance through the first few hours. But if the elderly person is wakeful in the early hours, this will not be very helpful. If a sleeping tablet has to be taken at bedtime for this purpose it has to be effective five hours later, which probably means a daytime 'hangover' effect. Others, to be taken on early morning awakening, might seem more appropriate but, unfortunately, these can produce an increased daytime drowsiness and perhaps confusion which only increases catnapping and, in turn, reduces sleep length at night. Carers can help in other ways such as creating the right atmosphere for a good night's sleep – a comfortable bed at the right height, warm, with a light covering, and a soothing, warm drink. She could also explain that everyone has a different need of sleep and there is no need to worry if the elderly person doesn't have those magical eight hours.

A healthy eating plan for the elderly should aim at a varied diet that balances the body's need for nutrients – the proteins, fats, carbohydrates, sugars and starches, vitamins and minerals which are the raw materials needed to repair the body. Often, elderly people will bruise easily, which may mean that they need more vitamin C in their diet: green vegetables, raw or lightly cooked, potatoes, tomatoes, citrus fruits or their juices should be taken daily. The B vitamins are important for strong nerves – they are found in offal, cereals, green leafy vegetables and bread. Bones break more easily in later years so vitamin D is also essential. It is a pity that we have lost the habit of eating oily fish regularly – herrings and sardines contain an abundant supply of this vitamin. Iron is the mineral needed to guard against anaemia and every carer should make sure her charge has enough by serving bread, potatoes, and green vegetables if he or she can't stand liver.

Fats are now indicted in heart disease so it is advisable to cut down on butter and dairy produce and choose alternatives to red meat like chicken, fish or pulse dishes; choose leaner cuts when you do serve meat. Sugar is nothing but a source of concentrated calories and can easily lead to obesity. At least try to cut down if not out by going easy on cakes, puddings, jams, marmalade and soft drinks. Fibre has become a household word, important not only for preventing constipation which may be an increasing problem with advancing years, but also keeping the bowel healthy and free from such diseases as diverticulitis, hiatus hernia and bowel cancer. There is no need to go overboard with bran; I found my mother did not tolerate it very well. More bread can be given, particularly wholemeal bread and potatoes. Choose a high fibre breakfast cereal and serve plenty of fruit and vegetables. Don't overcook and, again from personal experience, put out small portions – your charge can always come back for more.

Physical fitness is probably the best health insurance anyone could have. If the right kind of exercise is taken regularly it can improve the outlook and sense of well-being for the elderly; the body stays mobile, joints are prevented from stiffening and bones and muscles are strengthened. This can only be an asset, both for the cared for and the carer, for the elderly person will be able to be independent much longer. Moderate but regular exercise can also protect against diseases of the heart and circulation. Dr K. said he believes elderly people have over-high expectations of themselves; they want to continue as they have done in the past. I am inclined to think there is more danger in older people underestimating their physical capabilities. Exercise is essential in later life. As long as there is no serious health hazard, age alone should never be the reason for giving up an activity, or for not taking on a new one.

The choice is important: a stressful, competitive sport is probably not advisable. Exercising should create just a little breathlessness; brisk walking is excellent and swimming is the all-round sport which maintains stamina, suppleness and strength. Gentle yoga can be enjoyed by all but the very frail; it stretches the muscles, helps relaxation and encourages better breathing. Those who have practised yoga all their lives often seem to arrive at old age in much better shape, both physically and mentally.

Members of a Young at Heart club, which offers keep fit activities for the over-fifties, are discovering a new lease of life. Russell Robbins, who is nearing seventy, plays badminton, has a swim and goes for a gin and tonic before lunch. Then he dances away his afternoon. 'It keeps me happy and fit,' he said. 'I'm aiming to have the Queen send me a telegram when I'm a hundred.' Isobel Jackson and her husband play tennis and swim. They agree that their lives have become brighter since they joined the club and they both feel much fitter.

Looking after the elderly person's health means keeping the mind active as well. If they are to be an asset to the community instead of a liability, we need to discover new ways of making use of older minds. We shall also have to ask medical science to find ways of keeping minds in good health. Often a beautiful relationship continues between a parent and daughter, in spite of physical problems, because the elderly person still has a clear mind; he or she is still the beloved personality of earlier days. Conversely, and this is the tragedy when it seems to the carer, she may lose the relative because of deterioration of mental faculties. I shall never forget the tears in the eyes of the woman at one carers' meeting as she told me: 'I have lost my companion of fifty years; I feel so lonely, now.'

My indomitable correspondent Edna Smith directed me to some research which comes from the University of California's Department of Physiology and Anatomy. It has proved that not only can mental deterioration be prevented but that, even in old age, the human brain can develop and grow when it is stimulated by 'intellectual activity'. Roger Walsh, the Medical School's psychiatrist, has shown that an 'enriched environment' has stimulated changes in the brain cells of every species studied so far.

From the moment we are born, we begin to age. It is a biological process, an inexorable internal clock from which there is no escaping. Some people age more swiftly than others, which has something to do with our genetic make-up. If we come from a family with a history of longevity we are likely to pass our own three score and ten years, but it has also something to do with the way we live, which means that we also have it in our power to extend and enrich our life's span, independently of our ancestors. It is encouraging to know that human ageing has now become respectable as a field for scientific study. It is timely when we consider that this is something that happens to every one of us. If the quality of such research is sustained, it seems certain that medicine will learn to cope with things that go wrong, biologically, perhaps even psychologically, in the process of ageing. Research at the Weizman Institute of Science in Israel has produced a non-toxic compound known as AL 721 from egg yolks, which has reduced the viscosity of brain membranes of old mice almost to that of young mice, and it is hoped that some of the adverse effects of increased membrane viscosity in ageing human brains can be reversed, too. Viscosity of brain membranes is undesirable because it impedes the free flow of fluids, and hinders the functioning of the brain. A small number of elderly patients in an Israeli hospital were given AL 721 as a supplement to their diet, and they showed a marked improvement in health. Clinical trials are to begin in the USA before long.

It is the idea of what could go wrong which makes most people afraid of getting older. But normal ageing is a stage of life and not a disease. If we can realize this, the elderly person will achieve proper status at last and qualities like wisdom may be recognized again. As one journalist put it: 'I think that most ageing people would willingly put up with all the other inconveniences of old age in exchange for hanging on to their mind.' In his view, there is a need for more research on the ageing brain and the biochemical and structural changes associated with dementia, strokes and other aspects of ageing.

Ginseng has a very long standing reputation in China as a remedy for ageing. It has interested many Western doctors too, of late, including the gerontologist Dr Stephen Fulder, who has investigated it in the laboratory. He presented an interesting research paper to a symposium on ginseng, held in China. It took the form of a double blind clinical trial with ginseng on fifty elderly people. Dr Fulder pointed out that one problem seen in older people, especially in the Western World, is of premature functional impairment which shows itself in confusion, depression and a whole series of symptoms as well as degenerative conditions such as arthritis and cardiovascular problems. He carried out three types of tests: memory, awareness and concentration tests; tapping, auditory and visual reaction times; and a health questionnaire to measure mood and well-being. The study showed a clear improvement in those who took ginseng of 10 to 15 per cent in the psycho/physical tests but, Dr Fulder added, further testings might show that ginseng was possibly effective in the other areas. He described the complaint of the housekeeper of one of the patients, a 90-year-old man who had started to chase her round the room. They had worked together for fifteen years and this was the first time he had shown any sexual interest.

Often, old age is not the peaceful autumn of our years but a period of tension and crises, a time of necessary adaptation to all kinds of changes in lifestyle, brought about through retirement or bereavement. Habits and routines are important, for example, eating properly at regular times and keeping appearance and surroundings clean and tidy. Edna Smith has suggested several ideas which could give, quite literally, food for thought.

She says that cooking for one, or even two, is limiting and meals on wheels still means eating alone. One idea might be a cooperative effort like the four widows in Norfolk who each cook lunch for each other on Monday to Thursday. In Rotterdam, arrangements are made for older people who are beyond doing much cooking to have midday meals at a set price in the dining-room of a residential home, thus giving new friends to the residents and fresh air and good meals to the visitors.

There is a town in the USA where one of the biggest cafeteria-type restaurants had a different choice of 'pensioners' specials' on its daily midday menu at much reduced prices. They were appetizing, says Edna Smith, and well-balanced, and always included a side salad and roll. Help was available, too, if necessary, to carry the trays to attractively laid tables. 'And what about luncheon vouchers or an equivalent to be used as part payment at places cooking good meals which would take part in such a scheme?' she suggested.

She also advocates shopping aid, such as doorstep delivery of heavy goods by local shopkeepers. It is important, she pointed out, that there should be better display and arrangement of foods in stores, especially pre-packed meals for one or two, within reach of shorter people and with prices and instructions in bold print. 'Getting to the shops, or anywhere else, is sometimes difficult. There may well be a special bus or mini bus, or someone who works in or near the shop and could buy and bring back for frail people.' Edna Smith described the 'Vesper' scheme set up by Dr Snelgrove in Luton when stores re-opened specially one evening per week. Volunteers for care associations collected the frail and housebound, and those in wheelchairs. The shop staff came back, voluntarily, to push people around. 'Everyone took their time and had a marvellous evening – and shopped.'

The evening was obviously appreciated by those people's carers, too. However dedicated they are, most would agree that it would help if they could 'share' their elderly charge with just one or two friends. In a recent survey, it seemed that the quality of these outside contacts was more important than the quantity. Just one visit a week where the outsider really sat and talked and had a cup of tea with the elderly person was much more appreciated than spasmodic and uncaring visitors. There is all the difference in the world between being alone a great deal of the time, and feeling totally isolated.

Alex Comfort has said that people of all ages can feel lonely but many of those who have this distressing emotion in later years are people who are bereaved after being together for a long time with the person who has died. Illness also makes for isolation and loneliness. Of course, there are some people who stay alone from choice or habit, and they can be a great worry to their families and professional carers alike.

The once-upon-a-time 'good neighbour' is no more – if he ever existed – but there are some encouraging signs of neighbourhood schemes which have been launched by organizations like Task Force, whose work is geared to bring the old and the young together. Workers help local pensioners to set up groups to help themselves. They initiate the first meeting, finding the venues, producing posters and leaflets and then, generally, allow the pensioners to get on with it. In this way, they have promoted new branches of the National Federation of Old Age Pensioners, a pensioners' housing cooperative in Lewisham, a food cooperative in Paddington and a variety of clubs such as the Good Companions in Hampstead.

The popularity of that sentimental film *On Golden Pond*, with Katherine Hepburn and Henry Fonda fading among the autumn leaves, put old age on the map as a suitable subject for drama. Over the past few years, drama has been used to enlighten and enliven old age. Using the past experience of elderly people, various projects have been the source of creating drama and, in turn, stimulating the audiences to discover more memories and emotions within themselves. One of the leaders in this field is Pam Schweitzer, a talented dramatist, who, with the help of the GLC, put together *The Fifty Years Ago Show* based on memories she had gathered of life in Greenwich during the 1930s. Pam also involved herself in reminiscence work for the LEA: here, the minds of elderly people were stimulated by encouraging them to delve into their memories. Another Greenwich project, 'Shape', involving the Minnie Bennett sheltered housing scheme and the Greenwich Task Force, produced a booklet called *When We Were Young*, a collection of reminiscences that was distributed to two thousand housebound pensioners in the borough. There are plans for a follow-up in the form of a writing group organized for housebound people. Many carers have the sense that they and their charges live in two different 'time zones', where the elderly person likes to dwell in the past while her carer, naturally, thinks about the present and plans or fears for the future. By actively encouraging elderly people to recreate their past, the process can be positive for all concerned.

As Edna Smith said: 'Remember that in the American/ Canadian Indian culture, all agreements, treaties and negotiations were passed on orally, not in writing, and it was the duty of elders to ensure that these were passed on systematically, for if it was left to chance they would be lost completely in seven generations, as would the legends, history and culture. Seven generations! As a child, my grandfather told me stories of his childhood and his grandmother and only recently I was telling one of those stories to children who, by age, could have been my grandchildren. I realized that this was a seven-generation span.'

Much criticism has been levelled at television – that it destroys communication between people, sends minds to sleep. Personally, I found that it was a great comfort and source of entertainment for my mother who was not able to get out and about. It added another dimension to her life and kept her mind active. Some programmes, such as those with a self-help theme, can make a positive contribution to the quality of older people's existence. I am thinking of Claire Rayner's *Casebook*, and of her sensitive treatment of such subjects as bereavement. Sheila Innes, Head of Continuing Education at the BBC, has commented that television can and should capitalize on its non-formal approach to teach people at home. Her department produces around 250 new programmes each year, a key aim being to spark off new interests. If it is possible to persuade a fairly active person to go out and attend a class as well, there would be extra value in terms of the social and companionship elements. 'We know that although older people may learn more slowly, they usually retain specific knowledge longer,' she said. 'The worst feature of ageing is the attitude to intellectual capacity. When it comes to learning, chronological age does not matter.'

The Forum for the Rights of Elderly People to Education, (FREE) is committed to promoting and providing educational opportunities, both formal and informal, for older people in Britain. It is also concerned with the role of education in improving the social, economic, physical and cultural situations of the elderly. According to its manifesto: 'The fact is that more people than ever in historical experience are living to eighty and longer but there is minimal preparation, either for coping or enrichment . . . the claims of this growing section of the population for a fair share of the educational resources of the nation, to enable them to maintain an autonomous and fulfilling lifestyle, deserves recognition.'

A thriving and excellent movement, the University for the Third Age (U3A) represents education for the older person on a very broad scale. Organized on a national level, the emphasis is on self-help: it is the members themselves who decide on what they will study, and who will organize it. Meetings, tutorials and committees are organized within each area's group, which might number from ten to a thousand, and the teachers are drawn from this group, too. A great deal of the study takes place in the members' homes – there is no 'school' atmosphere whatsoever. Dianne Norton, executive secretary, says, 'It is based on the philosophy that older people have a lot to give, that they *can* organize themselves, and that they don't need someone to tell them what to do – it's essentially flexible.' There are now 130 groups across the country, and part of the recent large increase is attributable to fifteen new groups under the umbrella of the Third Age Project in South Devon.

U3A is no dilettante pursuit. As Sir Roy Shaw pointed out during the first annual Third Age lecture in September 1984, 'recreations' were not education and he hoped that U3A members would do a good deal of serious study to complement the work of the groups.

Another interesting development in this field is Third Age Radio. A grant from the Gulbenkian Foundation enabled a study to be carried out into the feasibility of local broadcasting by and for retired people. In a paper prepared by Deirdre Wynne-Harley a model scheme was outlined using CB Radio as its base. Along with a Third Age CB network, the author proposed a radio workshop that would serve older users and also have a community use, possibly in the form of a youth-and-age link. The proposal is to set up two pilot projects – one in Bexleyheath, involving the Bexley Association of Carers, and one in a Cornish village with a lively population of old people.

'What we want is training, training for organizing ourselves'; 'I'd like to do languages or poetry. I don't like sewing. I know what I'm like and I can't be the only one.' These two quotes from pensioners in the newsletter of the ILEA Education Resource Unit for Older People sum up the work the newly formed unit is trying to do. It outlines what it has done so far and appeals for more contacts, information and resources pertinent to their work. It also circulates a questionnaire asking older people to tell them about their experiences of adult education.

Dr Alex Comfort has described ageing as 'a peculiarly shaped social hat which can be taken off and jumped upon if the wearer doesn't like the look of it'. To judge by the increasing interest in Education for the Third Age it would seem that quite a number of elderly people are doing that.

I was interested to hear of the pioneering Outreach project in Southampton and its non-patronizing approach to education for the elderly housebound. The project was launched in 1981 when, with the encouragement of a local psycho-geriatrician, contact was made with and work begun at a private rest home. Soon, with a student on placement from university, a short reminiscence project took place resulting in a booklet on the residents' lives. The result has been a wide range of opportunities including crafts, music, local history, current affairs and quizzes. The essential element was that there were no prescribed courses, but the educational service was offered after residents had responded with their own ideas. They were in control of what they learned. As one resident said to a tutor: 'Please come back for another course. You don't talk down to us.'

The same sense of a project belonging to the people who use it exists at the Retirement Education Centre in Bedford. The library is manned by volunteers and books are chosen to complement courses. Each week, about forty different academic and practical subjects are on offer to students, who pay £10 a year to help with running costs. About four hundred of them attend the centre each day. The more recent sporting activities department has also become very popular. Arthur Barnett, who promoted the scheme, scoured Bedford for the use of facilities and there are now about five hundred retired people taking part every week in swimming, snooker, golf, table tennis, rambles, even riding.

The church has traditionally formed the backbone of life for the elderly, who, as well as helping to keep a place of worship serviced, have always formed a large part of the congregation and found solace and companionship there. Today however, there seems to be a much more ambivalent attitude in the church towards the elderly. Troubled by the falling off in congregations, some church leaders seem to feel that to encourage a largely elderly following will give an undesirable and negative image. Avril Watts found varying degrees of support when she contacted churches within the radius of her Age Concern offices. It does seem that at least in some parishes the spotlight is on the young, with all their problems, rather than the elderly, in order to present a more trendy image.

One church which has always responded and adapted to the changes in the life of the parish is the 900-year-old Bishopwearmouth parish church in Sunderland. Of those living near the church, 14 per cent are around retirement age and many are in need of support. In 1978, Age Concern visited the church, which sparked off an investigation into ways in which it could meet the needs of older citizens.

Existing schemes were also studied in York, Lichfield and Glasgow and it was seen that the church could become much more than just a meeting place for elderly people.

Equally important is for the elderly themselves to be able to contribute; we should tap their reservoir of experience and skills to the benefit of the community. At Bishopwearmouth, a Volunteer Bureau now alerts the retired to opportunities open to them on a voluntary or part-time paid work basis. There is also a counselling service for those involved in caring for elderly relatives. Part of the church has been converted into a restaurant which is open daily and where anyone can drop in for lunch, or a cup of tea. There is also an information desk which can refer people to other helpful agencies.

Age Concern is an admirable and very active organization which continues to initiate projects to help the elderly. In 1974, it considered the question of how old people were treated and what rights they have in society today. This sparked off a series of nationwide discussions on the subject. You need strength and political know-how to stand up and fight for yourself and this is precisely what many people in their later years do not possess. But their rights have been paid for, in advance, during a lifetime of work for their community and their families, in the rates and taxes that they have been paying for longer than any of us. It always annoys me – and I know I share this feeling with many of the carers with whom I have spoken – that many of the social services departments have a knack of making one feel as if one were begging. The truth is that society finds it easy to forget the debts it owes, and it has been failing to pay them back in full for so long that it has become used to thinking of 'the elderly' as a social problem and a drain on national resources. This is simply not true.

Some other countries treat their elderly so much better than we do in Britain today. I have written about the situation in Denmark; in the Netherlands, the old get half-price reductions not only on travel and museum entrance, as we do here, but on ballroom and folk dancing, cinemas, theatres, concerts, sporting events, the rent of holiday bungalows and all kinds of recreational activities including the use of tennis courts and bowling greens, even the hire of sailing boats, all of which is designed to keep senior citizens fully active in the community, alongside people of all ages.

'To go back to those mice,' said Edna Smith. 'They were old mice and if left locked in with their own age group, they died quite quickly. Stimulated by activities and alongside younger and female mice, they thrived, they lived much longer and they enjoyed life. It wasn't just existence. There is a lesson in this which is extremely apposite to circumstances in Britain, today.'

4. In Sickness

From time to time we hear about them; they are interviewed on television, or featured in a newspaper article: the men or women who are 'marvellous for their age'. And we wonder at their continuing ability to cope, to do all their own shopping, cooking, cleaning. Then there is the lovely old lady living in a rest home who, receiving the Queen's telegram of congratulations on reaching her centenary, is seen taking her usual tipple while she admits that she still has an eye for the gentlemen!

Almost without exception, I would say, these fortunate souls have been blessed with good and continuing health, a gift which only increases in value as the years go by. Granted, they may not have 'deserved' this in the truest sense of the word, not having taken particular care of themselves, but, as Dr K. suggests, have achieved it simply by possessing the 'right' kind of genes. Nevertheless, it does make all the difference between enjoyment of being elderly and merely supporting the burden of it.

We can be very positive when we speak of ageing that is free of disease. After all, it is the only stage in life when no one criticizes us for looking back and reflecting on what has happened instead of pressing forward to plan new activities. It could be a pleasant summing up; unfortunately, as our life expectancy has increased, so have the illnesses associated with advanced age. Inevitably, too, with this life-lengthening process, it will not be only the elderly 'cared for' person who has to face up to these problems but his or her carer, too – to the extent that her own life will be partially or wholly restricted.

Our carers are doing an excellent job in keeping the elderly from needing professional care, and in so doing, saving the country large sums of money. If only 1 per cent of those caring for an elderly person were to give up, the health and social service budgets would have to increase by 20 per cent overnight. It has been admitted that the success of any community-based care 'package' depends on a high level of commitment from informal carers. They often use their own savings to pay for the help they badly need. It has been estimated that those caring for the elderly at home are saving the statutory services something to the order of £5.3 billion every year. And when you compare the cost of a bed in a residential establishment, at upwards of £140 a week, with the maximum state Attendance Allowance, available only to the most severely disabled living at home, at £30.95 per week for day and night care, further anomalies are evident. There is another alarming fact: one in two carers are in poor health themselves, and most cannot easily seek treatment when there is no one to take over from them at home. The strain, as many carers have underlined, becomes almost intolerable.

Jean cared for her mother until she died, three years ago, and is now caring for a disabled brother who, at thirty-nine, is partially paralyzed. 'He can get about,' she told me, 'but there are so many problems involved, including financial ones. We would like to take him on holiday – we all need a break, but just cannot afford it.' Jean is now undergoing treatment for depression and, if the situation does not improve, it seems as if her husband will be taking care of her.

Kate and Michael became increasingly anxious about their mother, whose health is seriously threatened after prolonged caring for her husband. 'Dad has senile dementia and is incontinent although physically fit, but Mum has to do everything for him. She usually copes quite well but just after Christmas she was admitted to hospital. We began to worry she would snap if something wasn't done. Her family doctor hasn't been much help – just told her she was doing a good job and to carry on.' As one carer told me: 'No one realizes just what it is like to live with someone who has a disability twenty-four hours a day, twelve months a year. I feel, sometimes, I will kill him.'

I remember Graham telling me about his wife, Linda, who suffers from Parkinson's disease. Like many people, I believe, I was ignorant of the symptoms until I talked to him. These involve a curious flattening of the emotions and slowing of movement accompanied by rigidity and tremor. Nine out of ten patients become depressed and a progressive dementia, once thought of as a rare complication, often occurs. As the tremor and rigidity worsen, so movement becomes slower and more disordered. It is a distressing complaint, both for the onlooker and the sufferer, who may once have been very active, as Linda was. Now she is frustrated because she cannot do things; meanwhile, says Graham, 'she is driving me mad. She will decide that the airing cupboard should be cleared out so she pulls all the things on to the floor and then I have to put them all back. She wants to go out walking late at night, at eleven or twelve. She gets up and goes downstairs and turns on the gas fires without lighting them.'

Graham has become so fearful of possible consequences that for the last five months he has slept on a sofa, downstairs. His own health is beginning to suffer, too. Both these carers voiced that feeling of being just as frustrated as their charges when they realized what, once upon a time, they were able to do. Maybe their frustration is even worse, for they must somehow keep these feelings to themselves and find some way of lessening their own tensions.

It is sad that pre-senile and senile dementia seem to be on the increase. Several theories have been put forward to explain their onset. There is one school of thought that suggests it has to do with poisoning from heavy metals, another with diet. Both are progressive states and normally fatal, about five to seven years after the symptoms have first appeared. The development can be very upsetting, as Sarah experienced when she was involved with her partner's mother during the last two years of that woman's life. 'We still can't discuss it easily now, more than a year after she died,' she told me.

At seventy-five years old, Mrs W. began to demonstrate

signs of confusion. At first, this showed in small ways but gradually it became more noticeable and more frequent. Such confusion and loss of memory differ dramatically from the slow and partial loss of memory often seen in older people. In dementia the loss is sharp, a general rubbing-out of memories of the distant past as well as more recent ones. It can sometimes be complicated by dysphasia, where the sufferer seems to know what she is trying to say but cannot find the right word.

Soon Mrs W. was in an advanced stage of senile dementia. Sarah described her own anxiety and how she sought out magazine articles, desperately reading anything she could lay her hands on, on the problems of ageing parents. 'I looked for information in the library, I asked medical friends to explain the confusion of the aged to me. We were possibly luckier than some,' she added; 'two years is a comparatively short time to suffer the confusion of old age.'

Joyce remains in the throes of trying to cope with the developing stages of dementia. When she looks back, she remembers that her mother's confusion began to occur shortly after her husband died. She began to do odd things and although she and Joyce had only recently moved to the area, strangers phoned the school where Joyce worked to tell her that her mother was shut out of the flat and standing in the street. He daughter confesses she was ignorant of what was happening. 'I didn't know what to do because I had my job to hold down. I began to take Mother to the college so that I could keep an eye on her. I used to let her sit at the back of the class.'

It was not the ideal solution but then Joyce, like Sarah, did not suspect at once that her mother had a problem. Those early stages can easily be put down to 'old age', one of the reasons why dementia is often not diagnosed as such until it progresses. There came a time, however, when Joyce began to realize there was something very wrong. 'I suggested she might take an interest in making our flat cosy and homely, even cook for us both now and again. When I arrived home the following evening, there was a delicious smell of baking potatoes. The following evening: the same. I realized that this was the only thing she could remember to cook.'

Joyce took her mother to the doctor who confessed there was little he could do. Meanwhile, the older woman's condition deteriorated and she entered the stage which precedes incontinence, becoming slovenly and losing self-awareness. Increasingly, she needed Joyce's attention and the younger woman's work started to suffer, she became irritable with colleagues. About this time, she found a local day centre and thought this would keep her mother occupied for part of the day. But soon, there were more phone calls. Strangers told her her mother had 'forgotten' her key and was locked out. By this time, Joyce's life was cracking up: the man to whom she was very close died of a heart attack. 'I was too blinkered by my own problems to see it coming,' she said. 'It was then that I snapped. I got on a train and went to a friend who is a nun. She didn't say much to me about that night but apparently I spent most of it screaming. I got so tired, I kept passing out.'

Her mother continued to go downhill and Joyce remained, and remains, ignorant of how to cope with it. 'How shall I behave?' she demands. 'Shall I go along with the idea that there were carol singers at the door, last night? Shall I agree there is a crib in the living room? Do I dust round it or say it isn't there? And how big is it? Life size?'

Just as illness can sap vitality and isolate the sufferer so that he or she loses contact with friends, it can do the same to those who are caring for them. Yvonne is arriving at the point of breakdown as she views the 'vegetable' who was once her beloved husband. She has given up their shared dreams of a retirement spent travelling and enjoying life. She has had to say goodbye to the man she fell in love with because he could always make her laugh. 'It is hard even to have a conversation. I never know what he means. If he says "yes" does he mean "yes"? His memory has gone.'

I was impressed by one carer who contacted me. A

trained psychologist whose mother had suffered from senile dementia, Paulette brought insight to the period she spent looking after the elderly woman until she died. She is writing a handbook to give guidance to others in her situation. It contains many useful tips from the 'inside'. The first signs, she says, vary from one person to another. 'In my mother's case the first thing I noticed was that, although a keen gardener, she planted a rose upside down. She had dreams which seemed real to her, thought she had no money to buy food and started hiding what she had around the house.'

Her advice to carers in a similar position is: when something goes right or is enjoyed by the sufferer, however small, 'mark it up as a major achievement'. It helps, too, she says, to see the absurd side of things. An example of this was the time her mother put lipstick round her eyes instead of her lips as Paulette opened the door to a taxi driver. 'Some people feel resentment at the responses they get but, although understandable, this does not help anyone and only creates antagonism. My mother was aggressive for six months, but I always understood that it was not really her trying to break my arm – the part of the brain controlling aggression was being affected.' Once, she said, while they were out shopping, she found a packet of biscuits in her mother's quite small handbag, but had not seen it go in.

Repetition is one of the most frustrating things for such carers. It is impossible for the sufferer to stop asking the same thing. Paulette discovered a solution. She would reply to her mother once or twice and then produce a diversion such as television, or a flower in the garden, music which would distract the elderly woman.

'Remember how much worse it must feel to be so disorientated and to be caught in such a 'groove', even if the sufferer is not fully aware of it,' points out this compassionate woman.

She suggests that one should put out only that amount of food you want eaten at meal times. If the elderly sufferer sees a bowl full of sugar, she is liable to eat it all. Paulette did not have this particular problem with her mother, who went back to the childhood habit of hiding food and asking 'Where's Dick?', a Great Dane she had had as a child.

Paulette's mother loved toys, and a pink elephant, originally bought for a friend's child, became the faithful 'Pinky' – always there, as Paulette could not be, a friend or mother substitute. 'Although I took extreme care not to lose her,' said Paulette, 'it happened twice when I went to the Ladies. Once I ran out of the shop to see her going fast up the street, two hundred yards away, and the other time I found her in another department, urging everyone to look for me. After that, I talked to her continuously through the door. This could have been more of a problem had I been a man!'

Dementia is a dreadful illness for anyone to have and watching someone you care for struggling with it can never be easy, but there is no need to feel guilty if, sometimes, you become snappy, says Paulette. It is usually because you are overtired. Try to find someone to come in and give you a break away from it all, instead.

The increasing number of carers' groups which are springing up round the country do a valuable job bringing such people together, at least for a few hours, each week. They have a deep need for this release, for 'permission' to voice their grievances. At the meetings I have attended, there is an atmosphere of high anxiety, a bursting of the floodgates. When they go their separate ways again, it is obvious they have received support just by being together. One such group has been organized by home help supervisor, Rosemary Parsons, following the reports she received of its need. She has worked hard to get her group off the ground and is constantly involved in trying to obtain more funding to furnish her day centre. This will provide respite for carers while their charges spend some hours there, each week. Rosemary initiated and runs her group on typical lines: she encourages the carers to take on a part of the responsibility for its running, although that is not to say she can opt out.

'When you launch something like this, you give yourself a great responsibility,' she said. 'The carers come to rely on us for support, like one elderly man I have who attends regularly. He has been caring for his wife who has cancer, and managing very well. But this week, he broke down because she has had to go into a terminal care home.

'There are frequent crises – like the woman who finally snapped because she could no longer deal with her senile husband. She could not face up to the fact that it was useless to expect anything of him any more. When that time arrives, we have to assess whether it would be better for all concerned if he were taken into care.'

The meeting was a mixture of discussion about the day centre and the practicabilities of transportation, which is an ongoing problem. Then came the chance for everyone to have their 'say'. Dorothy described her husband, who was always active and the ideal handyman around the house. She has now had to learn to carry out all the tasks herself. She is also trying to persuade him to go to a day centre, but it is almost impossible. 'He screams at me,' she said. 'He's never done that in his life. We are both so frustrated. It is very difficult to know how far you can push people without upsetting them.'

Zena remembers her mother as a 'proper mum' but, finally, their roles were reversed. She is fifty now and cared for both parents before they died. Her father suffered a heart disorder and her mother was senile for twelve years. A typical day for Zena began early when she got her parents up and made sure they had a good breakfast before she went to work. Lunch might take three or four hours to get through while Zena persuaded her mother to eat. 'She also took to wandering and was found once miles away, with her feet raw from walking. And we'd be up till one or two in the morning, getting her to bed. She had a lot of strength and willpower. While Dad was alive, we'd undress her between us. The first night after he died, I had to push her down on the bed and put my knees over her to hold her down.'

Alzheimer's disease is a form of senile dementia that can

strike much earlier. It is sometimes suggested that a 'slow virus' is involved. In the usual viral diseases like measles, a virus invades a cell, takes over the cell's biosynthetic machinery in order to reproduce itself, and destroys the cell in the process. A slow virus is believed to invade the cell where it can remain for months, years even, until some unidentified trigger causes it to reproduce itself and destroy that cell.

June Polden has concerned herself with the problems of the disease and of those who care for its sufferers. She understands the mixed emotions, the sadness over a relationship which has changed to such a frightening extent, the guilt of losing patience, and the anger when the carer is tired. It was an inspiring experience to spend a day with June and her husband, Brian, when they invited me to sit in on their group. Their own story is a romantic one, for they met while Brian was caring for his elderly mother. He is a good-natured and cheerful man who had managed to put a brave face on for the outside world but June, visiting in the course of her work, read between the lines and saw his anxiety at not being able to cope. She took him under her wing and they grew fond of each other. They are now married and dedicated to their carers' group which supports people whose dependants suffer from Alzheimer's disease and other pre-senile and senile states. Besides the weekly meetings at a local nursing home, the Poldens organize holidays, such as a week on the Isle of Wight, which prove a respite for carers and cared-for alike. It was here that I spoke to several husbands who are carers. Alzheimer's disease strikes relatively more women than men but it is always a joint tragedy and I had haunting images of homes which had lost their heart because one partner lives in a world of confusion.

Kenneth told me that he found it hard to define exactly when his wife's problems had begun, although looking back, he can see all the signs. She became increasingly absent-minded and, a smoker, would put her cigarettes down everywhere, leaving a trail of burn marks. She deteriorated quite rapidly, would not bath and went to bed in the same clothes she had worn during the day. Kenneth was distressed by other changes in her personality: from being a loving wife she became a harridan, accusing him of taking the watch their son had given her. Later he found she had hidden it, another common trait of this illness.

Another husband, Harry, pointed out that it is because they just don't want to admit what is happening that the sufferer's nearest and dearest are the last to recognize the senile state. 'Other people have told me they saw the signs years ago, but I didn't notice them. At least she used to enjoy coming around the supermarket with me, to help choose what to eat. Now, even money puzzles her completely.'

Ingrid is a pretty woman in her fifties. Until five years ago, she and her husband lived a normal, happily married life. A virus infection put an end to this when Tom suffered brain damage and, subsequently, degeneration. Ingrid's doctors have told her the situation will never improve. She now lives with a man who is incontinent and incapable of carrying on an ordinary conversation; a man who thinks he is in his early twenties and unmarried. It seemed to me like a waking nightmare, a responsibility that many women would off-load onto professional carers. But Ingrid has stuck by Tom and refused to listen to any suggestion that he be taken into care. She has been out twice in the past two years and this only because of June Polden's encouragement. Her life is ruled by such events as Tom's incontinence programme; rather than interrupt this, she would prefer to have no respite from her caring role.

Not all the disabling problems of old age are as extreme, but are often the inevitable result of a weakening organism. As Dr K. has said, the ageing body may be likened to a car which is running down. But minor as they might be described in comparison with conditions such as cancer or stroke, they confront not only the cared for but the carer with real problems, and are sometimes as difficult for them to tolerate.

Incontinence sufferers find it distressing; it also perplexes the carers, who may not know how to deal with it. As Heather McKenzie has pointed out in her book *Take Care of Your Elderly Relative*, our society puts great store by bodily cleanliness and lack of smell; someone who becomes incontinent not only feels as if they have returned to infanthood but that their problem will make them a social outcast. Such an embarrassment may make the elderly person reclusive, because they are fearful they will not be able to cope in public. But anxiety can only exacerbate matters, as many of us know if we have ever suffered from nerves, and found our bladder working harder. Sufferers may try to conceal incontinence, hiding bed linen and underwear, and the carer may find it difficult to broach the delicate subject. It is possible that a third person, a doctor or other professional carer, will be needed to bring the subject out into the open so that something can be done about it.

Paulette evolved her own methods for dealing with incontinence as her mother's Alzheimer's disease progressed. As she says: 'The brain controls both emotional and physical activities, so the consequences of the disease may be as varied as aggression and incontinence. All Alzheimer's sufferers become incontinent in the end. When the problem first appears, a woman can use a sanitary towel alone. Waterproof pants may be required later on, but these are often plastic, cause condensation, rustle a lot and are not very comfortable.'

She recommends the use of Kanga pants with a wide Velcro opening. These may be obtained through the community nurse or the health visitor. When incontinence becomes a problem at night, a good rubber sheet is of immense help. This is better than plastic because it tears less easily and does not create so much condensation. As her mother's incontinence increased, she found it was better not to use a sheet on top of this rubber sheeting. Instead, she found the large size IPS Pant Liner Pads were useful – they were more comfortable for the patient to lie or sit on than the plastic-backed ones, and didn't cause such condensation. She also suggests that a woman's nightdress can be made much easier to handle if it is slit up the front and Velcro is attached to both sides. 'When the patient is in bed, the Velcro of the nightdress should be undone below the waist and the skirt folded up comfortably behind the shoulders. If one of a pair of Kanga pads is placed across the small of the back below the nightdress it will help to keep the nightdress dry.'

Shakespeare's 'seventh age of man' depicted the failing of the senses and the elderly person's sense of smell may be diminished so that he may not notice that the house smells unpleasant. His sensations of temperature may also be less acute, and hypothermia may develop. Our body temperature can fluctuate by as much as 1°C in a day. We 'run a temperature' when it rises above 37.5°C. If the body temperature is less than 35°C – way below the normal range – a doctor would diagnose hypothermia. As a rule when our temperature drops we are warned by our body's reaction – we shiver, we feel we should move. But because of the failure of the senses, older people may not have the same reactions so that, although it may seem surprising, they may be suffering an advanced stage of hypothermia without really being aware of it. Knowing this, many carers are fearful of leaving their charges for any length of time. Hypothermia or extreme drop in body temperature can be fatal, although people may be warmed back to their normal range of temperature. It would be advisable to call a doctor if a carer suspects that this is the problem. But in an emergency, or where you cannot get hold of the doctor, there are first aid measures you can take. First, you should make the room as warm as possible, but do not direct the heating onto the person. Unless he or she is fully conscious you should not give any warm drinks. It helps to get some more clothes on a hypothermia sufferer or to get him into bed with a hot water bottle.

MP Andrew Bowden has a long-standing interest in the elderly and their care. In his constituency of Kemp Town, Brighton alone there are 200,000 people of retirement age of whom 10,000 are comfortably off, and others have both their state and a private pension; there are some however who don't even know what is due in the way of extra benefits. In Mr Bowden's view, rather than make an overall increase, the government should concentrate on reaching this latter group in particular – the ones really in need of help.

He is a member of the All-Party Parliamentary Group for Pensioners, and has voiced his support for a 'cold alert' in winter, to focus attention on the dangers of cold to the elderly. In his view, and many others', they and those who care for them should not underestimate the dangers of cold. 'Those who were used to a cold home when they were young should remember that they are more severely affected by cold now, even if they don't feel it.' Some of his pointers for the prevention of hypothermia include:

Try to keep the sitting-room temperature as near to 70°F as possible.
Try not to stint on heating: heat the bedroom, at least a little, before you go to bed.
Wear several light layers of clothes as they will keep you warmer than do heavy thick clothes.
Eat little and often, although it may be an effort to cook; at least one meal should be hot.

Paulette also pointed out that sufferers from Alzheimer's disease can be kept warm by long socks over stockings and knitted wristlets which can be easily made, or cut off an old jumper to help to keep the hands warm. She also suggested that as the carer has often to leap out of bed several times in the night, it would be a good idea to sleep in a woollen pullover in the winter, using fewer bedclothes, as it saves time in reaching the patient and maintains warmth. It helps to wear a pair of pants, for the same reason.

Andrew Bowden mentioned that help can be sought for draught and damp proofing of a house by contacting the local council and any pensioners' groups or bureaux. Often, it is the fear of not being able to pay heating bills which causes illness, hypothermia, even death. The DHSS leaflet *Help with Heating Costs* gives details of the extra heating allowance, while fuel industries have a wide range of facilities which help make the quarterly bill a less formidable affair. The choice of heating should also be given consideration, so that the most suitable and economical method is selected. Here again, there is a leaflet from the Department of Energy called *Compare your Home Heating Costs*. Mr Bowden added that if there is trouble in paying the bills, it should be remembered that the gas and electricity authorities are not intransigent, and should be approached with the problem.

That excellent radio programme *Does He Take Sugar*? has illustrated clearly the attitudes of society toward someone who suffers from a disability such as deafness. It is echoed by Angela, whose mother was almost stone deaf for several years as well as suffering from poor near sight. Angela told me: 'What shocked me was how few people were prepared to write messages to her so that she could carry on a conversation. The stock comment to deaf people is, "Oh, it doesn't matter". That seems to me to veil either embarrassment or an "I can't be bothered" attitude. My mother was almost sent to Coventry by a lot of people. Surely they should have more imagination than to cut out the deaf like this.'

Because of these ingrained attitudes, elderly people may not want to admit that they do not hear as well as they once did, for fear of being rejected. Carers can help by making sure that when they are having a conversation with their charges, their faces are in a clear light. This is much better than shouting, which distorts the voice and can alarm or embarrass those who are hard of hearing. Sometimes, a hearing problem can be helped by having the ears syringed regularly; some people get a lot of wax in their ears. If the problem is more acute, it is possible to obtain a hearing aid on the National Health. It seems very unfair to isolate someone with a hearing problem just because 'they're old'.

We may perhaps be more sympathetic to someone whose eyesight is failing, but this doesn't prevent it from being as much an emotional as a physical problem, because of the innate fear of going blind. Carers would do well to reassure those they care for that while less than perfect eyesight may be a part of growing older, there are not that many who lose all their sight. Nevertheless, the alteration in lifestyle which follows an operation for cataract or the need for stronger glasses is not easy. When you can no longer do what you once did, nor read as much as you like at a time of life when you are less mobile, depression may result. When you cannot see very well you begin to feel anxious and less secure, and need comforting. Those who are caring for blind or partially sighted people may not know about the many benefits which are available, including the provision of 'talking books', which have been a great consolation to my aunt, whose sight is failing. She has been able to keep up with the news and 'read' now that she cannot continue with the needlework she used to love to do. The Royal National Institute for the Blind have an excellent leaflet, *Benefits for Registered Blind and Partially Sighted People*, which is available free on request from the RNIB.

It is a pity there are not more communities like the model Glavin District Caring Committee which Edna Smith has described to me, praising it highly. It was founded in 1974 with the express purpose of caring for elderly people and draws both its two hundred clients and its support from the eleven villages of north Norfolk, centred around the village of Blakeney. This has given the community conscience an opportunity to move into the caring field, and by cooperating the voluntary efforts of the villages, has provided the sources for the work. A local doctor and his team supply the professional back-up, providing not only an intimate knowledge of the needs and idiosyncracies of the people they care for, but an accessibility which is not otherwise available.

A part of the organization is a voluntary nursing service which includes SRNs and others. Some have a regular weekly task such as bathing the old person. They also help the district nurse with the management of acute illness and where necessary provide a night sitting service. These nurses have made a big contribution in the care of the old and ill in their own homes and have allowed several to die in their own beds rather than in the anonymity of a hospital. On two days each week there is a special caring service, when very infirm clients are collected from their homes and taken to the centre by volunteer drivers. Here they can receive treatment from qualified volunteer psychotherapists, be bathed by Glaven nurses and provided with coffee, lunch and tea while joining in handiwork and other sessions. Such a venture could profitably be copied throughout the country, to the benefit of carers and cared for alike.

5. Into Care?

However dedicated you are, there must come a time when you feel you cannot sustain your role any more and begin to consider a home of some kind for your charge. Unfortunately, past images of 'the work house' or being 'put away' linger obstinately, and there are many elderly people who announce, as one carer told me, that they would rather be dead. This is a pity because the new attitudes in homes are very different and there are many people who are making every attempt to change the old picture of people sitting round in a circle with their mouths open into a much more positive and involved existence.

As Heather McKenzie points out, no one can prescribe a rule which applies to all elderly people and all decision-making; she recommends total honesty and openness in discussing the 'home' option. 'To deny the elder the opportunity of involvement in decisions is to deny her a basic human right.'

This is complicated by the natural tensions which are a part of any relationship within a family. I found this with my mother. She resented any 'outsider' being brought into discussions and eventually – and in common, I know, with many other single daughters – I shelved the subject yet again and went on living from day to day. If you have talked the situation through, however, and all the options have been dismissed, or one has been chosen with which you do not feel happy, don't continue to agonize or feel constantly guilty. You must accept that you have done your best, that it is now their decision and they must be responsible for their actions. If their minds are made up, be supportive, not obstructive; if they are ill or confused and incapable of reaching a decision you may have to seek advice from a doctor, social worker or a specialist organization such as Age Concern about the best course of action.

Avril Watts commented that Age Concern would never recommend a specific home because the choice is very much an individual one, although if they heard a really bad report on one they would, of course, pass it on. 'You have to make your own judgement,' she said, 'and this should be based on several visits to the home. It is a good idea to go first on appointment and then casually.'

It is understandable that as the professional care structure of the elderly develops and becomes more complicated, the different kinds of homes can present a problem when you come to choose. It will depend, to a certain extent, on the amount of care your dependant needs. Sheltered accommodation might be an initial thought, designed for the elderly who are still quite active and capable of doing things for themselves, and wish to live autonomously. Each scheme involves an individual, self-contained home within a complex that is usually specially designed and built. They are warden-assisted, which means there is a responsible person on site, in case of emergency. The units are available for purchase or rent. You can find sheltered accommodation through local authorities, housing associations, charities or private builders. Laing is one such builder which also offers single person accommodation. Another, New Horizon Homes, a subsidiary of Algrey Homes Developments Ltd, specializes in private sheltered accommodation for the over-sixties. Elm Court is a typical example, with its thirty-seven one- and two-bedroomed flats with a resident warden on site, selling for a starting price of £29,500. Some of the special features incorporated in the complex include front door spyholes, low-sided baths with grab handles and emergency pull cords. There are rounded kitchen work tops with recessed handles to avoid knocks and bruises, and waste disposal units.

When I arranged to speak to the warden of a sheltered housing scheme run by local authorities on the south coast, I expected to meet someone much older. Joan Beckett surprised and impressed me. She has worked all over the world and brings a glamorous touch to the job with her blonde hair and casual clothes. She lives with husband, Roy, in one of the flats within the scheme and is in contact with all its residents by an intercom just outside her kitchen. If there is any problem or emergency, they simply press a button and are immediately in touch with Joan. 'Otherwise, I respect their privacy,' she said. 'I will only go in if there is an emergency or if I hear they haven't been seen about. We don't do any nursing – they have their own doctors call – but we make sure that they benefit from the various grants which are available, by putting them in touch with the various social services.'

Joan has a very good relationship with her 'old people', and is helpful and concerned – while she does not do shopping, she is ready to do small errands such as collect someone's prescription if there is no one else available – but she does her best not to become too sentimentally involved. 'It would be so easy to do that and I have to rationalize that they have had a good long life, most of them.' She keeps files on every resident so that she is aware of any health problems. Each morning, her first job is a routine call to each of the flats, just to see the occupants are up and about.

Her latest venture is to initiate a residents' association aimed at bringing everyone closer together. A programme of bring and buy sales, coffee mornings and coach outings is being arranged. Now that it is launched, Joan has left her 'old people' to run it for themselves, all part of her philosophy to encourage them to be independent.

She wishes people would realize how pleasant this kind of accommodation can be. The flats are light, bright and centrally heated, often almost wholly paid for by the local authorities. 'Elderly people do adapt,' she said. 'I had one lady who had lived in her house for fifty-seven years and didn't want to move, but within two weeks she had settled in happily.'

The number of people of pensionable age in this country is still rising steeply. The Anchor Housing Trust has been aware for some time that there is need to provide very frail, elderly people with more help than can be given in the community or a sheltered home. This need is also bound to increase over the next twenty to forty years. In spite of this the Trust's philosophy is still to encourage maximum independence. Residents in their homes have their own furniture and things about them. They are encouraged to provide some of their own meals and to have visitors and as much contact with the outside world as possible.

Sheila Hoe, resident manager of Highfield House, Anchor's first scheme, said that these homes fill a much-needed gap in the care structure for frail, elderly people. They include a flat for those who want to come in for a short period in order that their families can go on holiday, and additional provision is made for older people who suffer from mental frailty. The Trust is facing financial problems, however, because of the sharp cut in public funding even for priority groups like the very elderly. They must find £50,000 for each scheme, and so far have been able to continue to build only by combining private finances such as building society mortgages with charitable gifts.

Faced by the problems of deciding where the cared for shall go, probably the last thing the carer wants is to have to cope with the finances, but this is imperative, as Isobel pointed out to me. She was brought up by her aunt, whom she loved 'more than anyone in the world', and said that she felt the lessons she had learned were vital. 'As soon as possible, the relative who is taking care of the frail or ill person should arrange to have Power of Attorney through a solicitor, which costs about £15 to £20. When the person is only mildly affected they know who they want to take over their affairs and can willingly sign a document. The symptoms of senility include illogical suspicion, and if the person reaches that severe stage in the illness, they will not sign and then you can't help them.' Isobel was able to take over all her aunt's affairs and pay all the bills with money the elderly woman did not realize she had.

Mary Blair of the Money Case Work Bureau agreed and suggested that at this stage the carer should also make sure there is a reasonable will. Solicitors will visit so that this may be drawn up. 'Try to make sure this is done before mental deterioration, while the elderly person knows their own mind.'

Mary is also perturbed by a problem that was once the concern of only the very wealthy: inheritance. She described a typical case of a mother and daughter living in the mother's house. 'If she has to go into permanent care, the property would be sold and the proceeds go towards payment for that care. Do you transfer it into the daughter's name and when do you do it? There needs to be some counselling on this subject. In the past, a property was properly tied up for those who were rich; now it could be ordinary people who experience this problem – "children" living in a council house, for example, who have been promised their share of the family home.'

The television film *Health or Human Rights – A Happier Old Age?* spotlighted the lack of adequate caring facilities when it showed elderly women like Gwen Mercer in a local hospital in Hove because there was no one to look after her. At least she received proper medical attention, but there are thousands living in squalor without adequate help. Hove has a large number of rest and nursing homes – forty-nine in one square mile – and East Sussex has more than eight thousand beds for the elderly. Fees are not cheap – some pay up to £250 a week, although the average is around £150 – and the film described private health care as a booming local industry. According to some in authority, the standard of care in these homes is adequate; others, however, such as an auxiliary nurse called Julie who works in a private home, said that the patients are deprived, in her view, of good care. Another district nurse said that some people go into nursing homes without anyone giving a professional opinion on the state of their health. It seems that although the priority is to develop domiciliary care, many old people still slip through the welfare net.

This echoes Rosalind's experience, who suggested to the GP that her partner's mother needed a short stay in hospital 'to get her into a healthier state and so that they could clean her up'. His response was, 'We can't take just any old dear into hospital.' A fall and fracture precipitated her admission and the three arrived at the local casualty department one evening. From then on, as Rosalind described, the situation altered.

'The sister in charge was very kind. While the old lady was being X-rayed and bandaged she had a word with us and remarked that it was obvious we needed help. They had taken off seven layers of top clothes and put her into fresh hospital underwear. They also cleaned her up as much as they could. She told us we were entitled to daily visits from the health visitor, bathing staff and an arrangement for a home help to go shopping. Significantly, she added that these arrangements "carried far more weight coming from the hospital".'

It took an emergency for Rosalind to obtain this desperately needed help. But as it turned out, it was never brought into use. The next day the old lady collapsed and returned to hospital, where she stayed in a ward for seven days while staff tried to restore her health. 'They were very kind although she was particularly difficult to nurse.' Later, she was moved to a geriatric ward with the idea that she would stay another month in hospital and then have short-term stays in a special geriatric unit to give Rosalind and her partner an occasional break. But the old lady died after a week, and the strain of this experience still haunts Rosalind.

'If anything can be done to allow people to have comfort and dignity in their last years, it is of utmost priority,' she said. 'It's a pity this elderly person did not have more time in the geriatric ward, where she was very peaceful and calm for the last week of her life.'

Joyce's mother was still at a relatively early stage of dementia when Joyce met a woman who had registered her home as a residential care home. Her mother went there 'just for a holiday' and Joyce suffered a lot of guilt at the beginning. But it soon seemed as if this was the solution to her problem, allowing her to work with peace of mind during the week, bringing her mother home at weekends.

As the elderly woman's condition continues to deteriorate, Joyce has begun to wonder how long this solution will continue. 'She is dreadfully disorientated when she is with me. Last weekend, she had a stomach upset and couldn't remember where the bathroom was. She wanders at night and I know that if this develops, the present home will not want to keep her. She will need total supervision.'

In the meantime, Joyce has financial struggles. She applied for a supervisory grant and receives £19 a week which goes straight into payment for the home. They are now using up her mother's savings and Joyce is anxious as to what will happen when these are gone.

As I have said, there is a wide variety of residential care homes, run by local authorities and private or voluntary charitable organizations. It is important to check them individually, as some horrific tales have been told of the 'cowboy rest homes', which offer a raw deal to the elderly. As a member of the caring profession put it: 'Some are excellent. But many are just a charter for despair. Unfortunately, it is very easy for a failed hotel proprietor to jump on the lucrative rest home bandwagon with no experience and very little to stop him.'

Local authority rest homes are for people who, because of their age or infirmity, are in need of care not otherwise available. They do not offer a full-time nursing service, and the average age of residents is usually over eighty. The charges vary according to district but are usually in the region of £95 a week. There is possible help from the local authority or DHSS for those who cannot afford the fees. Voluntary and private care or residential homes are also suitable for those who do not require full-time nursing. The cost varies considerably and if the carer or cared for cannot meet them, they may apply to the social services department of the DHSS.

'Don't leave it too late,' was the advice of Mrs Jean Bridle, secretary of a branch of the East Sussex Residential Care Home Association. The Association wants to see an embargo put on unregistered homes where they think the elderly could be at risk. It insists on high standards and a homely and caring environment, and thorough inspections are made before a home is accepted into the Association. 'The first things we look for are the care and friendliness of staff, how they respond to residents' needs and how much attention they pay to little things,' said Mrs Bridle. 'Then we look at the facilities: are they adequate and clean, and are the meals wholesome and nutritious?'

Mrs Bridle considers that 99 per cent of all homes offer good standards, but she is concerned for the future because of government cuts. The Association has noticed that some applicants for rest homes are by then more suitable for nursing home care, though it believes they could have benefited from rest home care had they been encouraged to enter one earlier. Many elderly people tend to hold on to their homes too long, she believes. Sometimes, they are persuaded to do so by the social services, but the Association believes they can go downhill much faster in their own homes.

There are some points any carer should ask herself when she has made that first inspection visit. How experienced are the staff and is there a high turnover? How many staff to a shift, particularly a night shift? If a resident falls ill suddenly or is particularly frail or incontinent, will she be asked to make other arrangements? Are the residents encouraged to do as much for themselves as they can? What are they doing when you visit? Stuck in an armchair, staring at television, or active and alert? Try to visit the place as often as you can, at different times, so that you can get the 'feel' before you commit yourself. What about money – how does the home handle your charge's money, including any special allowances he or she receives?

For many reasons, in particular my own preconceived ideas, my recent experience with my mother made me apprehensive about visiting a nursing home. The memory of her death in such a place continued to haunt me but I knew that I must see inside one if I were to understand better the subject I was writing about. I chose a private nursing home, situated in a wide, leafy avenue opposite a park. As I walked toward it, it seemed to me a classic setting. Matron greeted me and was at first brisk and professional but later, as we spoke, she became gentler and I realized, as I have realized many times in the course of interviews, that professional carers must sometimes wear this mask simply for self-protection. Most of the patients were geriatric, coming from rest homes because they now needed nursing care; the youngest was a lady in her sixties who was crippled with arthritis and whose daughter could not cope as she had three children to look after. Two other residents were confused and incontinent and one suffered from diabetes.

Matron said that many of their families experience guilt in bringing their dependants to a home but she tried to reassure them that if it had reached the point where day and night care was necessary, they were right to seek help. Her oldest resident had been a woman of a hundred who continually discharged herself, until she had to admit that she could not cope any more. Residents at this home have a private room, or they share with one another, and a television set appears to dominate most of their lives.

'We don't have a dining-room because they are inclined to squabble about their chairs,' Matron told me, 'so we serve their meals in their rooms and they can visit one another.'

The day is punctuated by meal times. It begins early with breakfast between six and eight, then everyone is bathed and dressed by 10.30 a.m. when they have morning coffee or tea. Lunch follows at one and afternoon tea is served before their evening meal between five and six. Many of the residents are in bed by eight, although there are some who like to stay up and watch television. Hot drinks and biscuits are available before they go to bed. 'Being here prolongs their lives,' said Matron. She added blithely, 'They've got warmth and food.'

'. . . and not much else,' I added to myself as we toured the place: a woman suffering from multiple sclerosis whose bed sores after a hospital stay had made her feel, she said, 'old for the first time' . . . the strange little scrap of a woman being visited by her sister who had cared for her and all her other sisters. Once, the family had been well off, living abroad . . . or that confused person who wandered up and down the hall as though looking for a way out. The visit disturbed me: it brought home to me once again the realization that whatever the situation and however much money is available, when you are elderly and ill there is not much quality left in life. Professional carers like Matron, who was obviously a kind and giving person, can only give so much. I am reminded of a friend of mine whose mother is in an excellent home but who, suffering from Parkinson's disease, is unaware of this care, unaware of her daughter who visits her regularly 'just to sit with her, unable to communicate, just hoping she knows I'm there'.

At one point, my mother had to spend some time in hospital. She hated hospitals and was reluctant to go. However, she was fortunate in being placed in a small 'cottage '-type hospital where the doctor sorted out some of her problems and she returned home with a new lease of life. Sometimes, the benefits of a hospital stay can be negated because of lack of care facilities on the elderly person's return home. Edwin Fordham and Barry Gilbert came up with one idea after they met an elderly woman who was worried about being on her own after returning home. They invented the BEF electronic alarm, which works by being 'told' three times a day that its owner is safe and well. In response to a bleeping sound set for morning, lunchtime and evening, the owner must press a button on the unit. If he or she fails to respond, a bell fitted to the outside of the house will sound, alerting neighbours and passers-by that help is needed. It is a godsend to people like the woman who fell and broke her arm, then lay there for three days before she managed to catch the attention of a boy delivering leaflets. It is something Avril Watts feels is vital if domiciliary care is to be encouraged.

Aftercare when an elderly person has left hospital can make all the difference between recovery or not. A Community

Health Council report, *Who Really Cares?*, written by Val Williamson after interviews with patients, found that 10 per cent of pensioners had no visitors at all during the first two days after returning from hospital, and for those who did receive company the most frequent callers were relatives, friends or neighbours, the majority of whom offered company, rather than help with household chores or nursing.

There is the need for a routine check about home circumstances and aftercare needs. The report suggested a minimum of twenty-four hours' notice before discharge from hospital, and a visit by a member of the primary health care team within two days of this, if the patient is over seventy-five and living alone, with a follow-up a month later. Written instructions should also be given to the elderly person before he or she leaves hospital on how to take medicine, and on services to be provided, along with a list of useful telephone numbers and addresses. A hospital discharge letter should also be sent to the GP concerned within twenty-four hours. Alan Brookes, secretary of the Community Health Council, called the report a 'pioneering piece of work'.

The decision as to whether your elderly dependants should go into a home or hospital weighs heavily with many carers. Ellen's story was on a much lighter note. Her parents had discussed the subject ad infinitum and had come to the conclusion, feeling they could not cope much longer, that they would put their house up for sale and go into a home. They duly booked themselves in and then 'a sort of homesickness developed. Every day, they would have their breakfast and then catch a bus and go back to the house. They would have a picnic there and stay until the evening before returning to the home. They were most ingenious in coming up with all kinds of reasons for their absence.' After a week or two, Ellen confronted her parents and suggested that they really didn't want to go into a home at all. They agreed, and took the house off the market.

'Someone said to me: "You can't make their decisions for them; they must live their lives the way they want to,"' she said. 'It's taken a weight off my shoulders.'

6. Till Death Us Do Part

I began to write this book a few months after my mother's death and since then, in talking to carers both informal and formal who have reflected my thoughts and feelings, I have reached a greater understanding of what caring for someone requires. I have realized that I was not always prepared to make the sacrifices it demands and, consequently, can now identify the conflict of emotions that I experienced during the last years of my mother's life.

As I have written already, the situation 'at the time' is usually ill prepared-for, there is no counselling available, it is not possible to have a rehearsal. It creeps up on you so that, as one carer told me, you do not reflect but 'live each day as it comes – there is no point looking to the future'. Perhaps if we carers were more able to face up to the future which, by its very nature, must result, sooner or later, in death and the carer's release, the whole thing might take on a different perspective. We could accept it 'for the time being' instead of looking on it as a life sentence.

It is useless to say this, I know, but I wish that I could have understood that then – and not now, with hindsight. I feel I might have behaved differently and many carers, I know, feel the same. But when you are in the thick of the battle, it is hard to see things clearly. I was racked by emotional conflict and although I recognized some of the feelings – the frustration, helplessness, the anger sometimes, the guilt – I could not really understand my reactions at times to the situation that was going on. I said things, did things which were not 'me' at all. And I know from my conversations with other carers that I was not alone: in their various ways they have described or implied they shared this feeling of being 'in bondage'. Carers, especially those who have cared for an elderly parent for a number of years, rage against being trapped, seeing time passing by and the options lessening. Some of them find this very strong emotion only comes to the surface when the cared for person has died. Every one of us is different; my anger spent itself during those last years. I got absurdly angry over very little things, for example if someone didn't come up to scratch over something I, or we, had asked them to do. I would reach the point of screaming with anger about them but really, I know, I was screaming to be set free.

The two key things which have begun to help me towards this understanding have been an interview with Jenny Symons, who is a counsellor for Cruse, the society which supports and counsels bereaved people, and Dr Tony Lake's book *Living with Grief*. Both of them have spoken to me of the nature of grieving and brought me to the surprising realization that mine, for my mother, began some time before she died.

Anyone who cares for an elderly person knows inherently that both of you walk in the valley of the shadow of death together. Even if your charge is hearty and healthy, there is still the sense of remembrance of things past, rather than the present vitality of a woman living with her young children. There is a pervading sense that you are helping someone to prepare for dying, and sometimes this can be very depressing. I can remember many a night when I lay awake, torturing myself with thoughts of what the event might be like, of how frightened I would be, and, eventually, crying myself to sleep. And I had a curious experience one evening, something like a premonition, when I 'saw' my room bare of furniture.

I know, too, that I share my distress with many other carers when I remember the occasions I was told, 'I'd be better off dead so that you can get on with your life,' or 'Well, I won't be here much longer.' I know that they will understand my feeling of failure that, after all, I had not given the solace, had neglected the care that was needed. There were other withdrawals which I found hurtful, when the lack of contact made it seem the misery was too great for me to come near.

Whatever work I had to do during the day, I tried to make a point of sitting with my mother after our evening meal, but often when I tried to make conversation she seemed to prefer to watch television. There was the sense of a barrier, of a partial loss of the person I knew. For a long time I hated television and its capacity to create these barriers in communication. It is only recently that I have recognized it is 'company' now and again. There were, of course, other times when I rebelled and decided I simply would not try any more! I felt so frustrated and angry because I knew that it was not possible to live my life fully as long as this sad responsibility was there. I felt angry with my mother for becoming old because our relationship could no longer be as it once was. Anger seems to have been one of my strongest emotions, then – *now* I feel purged of it.

Long before her death, therefore, I realize, I was trying to come to terms with our relationship, trying to summon up strength to cut myself free so that I could have a separate existence – yet I knew, when it came to the point, that I should never leave her. At the same time as this longing, I would feel tremendous guilt for feeling it, and I knew how hard my grief would be to bear, should that 'release' ever come about. My grieving had begun, even though I might not have recognized it as such, a long time before we were actually parted by death.

Anna frankly admitted her longing to be free at all costs when she said: 'I can't communicate with her. It's like living with a vegetable. I wish I could come down one morning and find she had just died.' She thinks frequently of what she would do then – pack up the house, go on a cruise, go to America for six months . . . 'I plan, yes, but I don't know what I would do, really. I am so conditioned. No one really understands the experience unless they have lived with it.'

Her sense of isolation, of living with someone who is becoming increasingly dependent on her until she cannot call her life her own was a *leitmotif* in carers' conversations. If there were any need of justification for helping such carers financially it is that at least in one respect it could ease the constant struggle. There is no more deserving cause, in my opinion, than this forgotten army of carers who soldier on, putting a 'brave face' on it all so that their desperation is never really recognized.

Anna described a carers' meeting when a young social worker came to address them. '"You must get the doctor to be interested," she said. I burst out laughing. My doctor wouldn't even come out when someone was sick. "You mustn't feel alone," she said. How can you not feel alone? The only time this problem was coped with properly was when you were part of a large family and everyone mucked in.'

That one-time nuclear family which stayed together as a part of a closer community gave us an education in grieving, suggests Dr Tony Lake. In such communities, he points out, grief was more public and it was shared. People probably did not live as long, so death and the grieving that followed were more often experienced and better understood. Today, he says, we face the problem of knowing little about grief until it is upon us. 'We are confronted by the prospect of having to grieve with inadequate preparation. We must find another way,' he writes.

Sometimes, it seemed to me, the imminence of death in the household affected the carer far more than it did her parent, who might not realize – perhaps because of senility – or might choose not to recognize that he or she was close to death. As Anna told me: 'Mother is fine. She'll go on to be 103 but I don't know if I can cope that long. She is in a better state than I am.' Oh, the weight of emotions behind her statement – ones I recognized well: the frustration of her own life moving on, resentment at the drain caring had become!

Pauline sensed a cloud of doom and gloom hanging over the sitting-room. She admitted that even though it made her feel guilty, she could not bring herself to sit in the same room as her mother throughout an afternoon, because of the depressing effect it had on her. Other carers seem to be able to shoulder it all and, apparently, remain cheerful. 'I am always amazed by women and how they put up with things,' commented P.M., 'and how wonderful they are – the only superiority men have is physical strength. Women can be just as intelligent and even more dedicated.' Although she told me she had had her 'tearful days' I could not imagine P.M. anything less than the bubbly person I saw.

It is not always in their best interests for carers to present this bright and stoical front to the world, this air of being able to cope with the dying. Carers need support if they are going to ride the storms of this period. I can remember several occasions when I felt so weighed down with the anxiety of one medical problem after another that I decided I would blurt it all out to our GP. I would tell him how I felt – at the end of my tether – and how the atmosphere was getting under my skin and depressing me, making me ill, too. But what was the use, I asked myself? And as another doctor, a psychologist, said to me, I knew I had two options: to be selfish and go my own way, or stay and see it through. If I really questioned myself, I knew which one I would choose.

I made an effort to keep myself physically healthy, however, and it is advice I would offer any carer. Eat well, get some exercise and fresh air, do not let yourself get run down – things seem ten times worse if you do. Where the emotional and mental stress-ridden side is concerned, there are no such simple answers. Although many of the carers to whom I have spoken seem to manage to put on a brave face, they should recognize that in travelling toward the inevitable destination with their charges it is perfectly normal to feel depressed, dispirited, frustrated – angry. This last emotion, which seems the most unacceptable to many of them, is a natural part of our basic instincts – of our sense of survival. But because it seems 'selfish' to have this feeling I know that many, in common with myself, thrust it aside or try to convince themselves that it is directed at something, anything other than the person concerned.

I recognized this behaviour in myself. I heard myself say things which were hurtful, which I did not intend to say, and for which I knew I would feel guilty, later. There are carers who have felt like being physically violent towards an elderly person who is being particularly aggravating, or who is sapping their morale. If you reach this point of anger and despair, you should not try to 'grin and bear it', but go for help and let the person you ask for that help know just how tense and tired you are. The Samaritans are a wonderful support group, but it is important to take action before you reach the stage of needing their help. And a knowledge of the ageing process, basic home nursing skills and support services also helps to prevent you from reaching this stage. It is now more generally recognized that those who look after the elderly cannot and should not be left to battle on alone. Their health must be maintained both for their own good, and for the good of those they care for. You should take care of your own needs, learn to recognize the difference between caring for a person and loving them. And the ability to put tasks and emotions into compartments, and to create a further compartment where time is allocated for the carer's own needs, can avert the nervous exhaustion from which so many suffer.

I managed to do some of the things I wanted to, when I wanted to, while my mother was alive. I tried sometimes to please myself, reasoning that I was not being selfish but taking care of myself, body and soul, in order to be stronger for us both. I did my daily exercises before our evening meal, and after I had finished writing for the day, which is when I like to exercise, even though my mother occasionally grumbled about the meal being later than she liked. I recognized, too, that a certain routine was comforting in the face of her constant anxiety, so I tried on the whole to stick to one.

Friends knew that I would go out with them later in the evening, when we had had our meal, and that I had to make arrangements for her to go to my sister's house if I was going to be away from the flat for some time. I sometimes became very emotional over her part in the caring routine, feeling that I was being smothered. Late at night I would feel all my anger mounting inside me and pick up the telephone to make a furious call to my sister demanding that she help me, do more, give me some time for myself. I felt very bitter toward her – jealous, I suppose, of the fact that she had married and had two children. I have explained how, since our mother's death, our relationship has improved and we are now getting to know one another again as two adult people who, despite our very different lives, can now find more things in common than ever before. According to Dr Lake, this is often the case after a parental death when the family structure is reorganized and a different pattern emerges.

While one's parents are still alive, and if one does not move on to the next stage in life – marriage, for example – there is something of the Peter Pan syndrome about the 'children'. I have seen this in myself and in several of the carers I have spoken with. Since my mother died I have felt changed, diminished, recognizing my own mortality, coming to terms with myself slowly, and I feel that, painful as it is, I am now 'growing up' for the first time in my life.

During those last years I felt isolated, in a special place with no reference to the outside world; something that Dr Lake urges should be resisted. If we allow ourselves to be cut off from the people who care about us, if we withdraw from our rightful place in the world, we may never be able to reclaim that place as our own, he points out. How often during these past months have I felt exactly that, and been reminded of the story of the 'boy who never grew up' and who tried to return, only to find the window was barred against him. How often have I shared this feeling with other carers: 'alone without my best pal' as one said, 'unable to start all over again'. The world has carried on without us and it is hard to join in again.

Another point which Dr Lake makes is the need to resist dependence. 'You alone must be in charge of what you think, what you feel,' he writes. It is important not to allow anyone to treat us as their object, precious though that may be, or we shall become less of a person in our own right. There is a need, he says, to be ourselves and not the property of somebody whom we have to please. We need freedom to do, think and feel what is right for us as individuals. Then if there are compromises to be made we know where we stand and how far we can go.

There are many parents who, perhaps unconsciously, will use the special bond with their carer as a tool. They may arrive at dominating the carer's life to the extent that they 'order', not ask, not to be left alone. 'Promise me you'll never put me into a home,' or 'Don't leave me. Promise me you won't leave me.' And if the command is disobeyed, they suggest, the consequences will be dire. Such emotional blackmail, because that is what it is, can be very stressful to the carer who, although she needs respite from the battle, fears to go out in case the elderly person dies on her own. The anticipation of the guilt she would feel if there were an accident or a death while she was away is like the ladybird in the nursery rhyme.

We all need something to ease the tensions, however, and so we find some more acceptable 'escape'. In my case, I resorted to exercise in an almost compulsive way and, on occasion, drank more than was good for me in an effort to relieve the pent-up emotions inside me. I know I shared with many others the sense that most escapes were going to confront me with more conflict, more stress. The demands on time and energy, the inability to evade a sense of being trapped, leads many carers to use alcohol as an escape. I was possibly luckier than some. I can imagine that for someone who is totally isolated from any kind of social life, what begins as the only way to escape for a brief period could become an alcohol problem, over time.

Guilt is a destructive and negative emotion. I think of that carer who was so distraught after she had decided to put her mother into residential care and give up her own caring role. She felt guilty because she had wanted to be relieved of the role, because she wished to teach 'properly' as a way of life instead of having to be content with supply teaching, and because she was asking someone else to take over her responsibility. For a while, she could not face herself or the situation, to the point where she could not even visit her mother. When, to assuage this guilt, she decided to bring her mother home, it was in the knowledge that there was no prospect of the type or intensity of the demands changing; on the contrary, they would only be exacerbated by time and her mother's deteriorating health.

'Care of the invalid has one virtue,' comments Mary Gordon in her sensitive book *Final Payments*. 'One never has to wonder what there is to do.' Yet this attitude could line up problems for the future of many carers. If their lives become restricted by the demands of the person for whom they care, and lonely because of the virtual social isolation that these demands have imposed, what will happen when that relative dies? There will ensue such loneliness, exacerbated by their inability to find their way back to their rightful place, their belief that now they have no real purpose left. Heather McKenzie urges: 'It is essential to keep in contact with people and not become completely immersed in the care of the aged person.'

Nevertheless, you have to find some kind of lifestyle which will carry you through the present as well as leaving your future options open. As one carer said to me: 'You must say to yourself, This is my life as it has to be lived at the present time. I won't regard it as being wasted years. I will take pleasure from those hours of freedom I may have. I will say to myself that what I am doing is worthwhile.'

Paulette filled me with admiration when she described how she coped with the deterioration and imminent death of her mother. Her behaviour was almost saint-like and in sharp contrast to my own, I felt. She was aware of exactly what she was taking on when she moved the elderly lady from the west country to London. 'My advice to carers is, don't waste energy worrying about the next day or further, but do keep at least one interest of your own so that you can think about other things that interest you while you care. I chose courses with the Open University, but any hobby you like, be it gardening, stamp collecting or reading would be effective, provided you keep it up and think about it a lot.'

As for myself, although I continued my work throughout that time, I found it hard to keep things in compartments, as I was constantly anxious and stressful, aware of 'time running out' and, with this growing awareness, a simultaneous reluctance to face up to it. Death has always terrified me: from early childhood I have been at once fascinated and horrified by it. I find it unthinkable that life can be extinguished in a second, but I regret that I never broached the subject with my mother. I feel that she, too, was aware of its approach and that we entered into some kind of conspiracy whereby it would not be mentioned. But it stalked the flat, nevertheless. When I spoke to Jenny Symons about this, she said she felt it was helpful to talk about it and that, for the carer, it was often valuable in initiating the grieving process before the death. But people differ in how they confront their own death, she pointed out, and it is sometimes difficult to make that initial move and bring it to the surface. 'The most anyone can do is to make overtures and allow the subject to be picked up if the other person wishes.'

Often, attitudes towards death – either confronting our own or that of those who are near to us – will be influenced by whether we have developed some philosophical or spiritual acceptance of it. Because of my own somewhat ambiguous feelings towards any kind of afterlife I have sometimes felt hurt by the attitude of clergymen and priests with whom I have spoken. I found that they did not offer me any kind of comfort for the feelings I was experiencing. Then I reasoned that our attitudes were different – they had total faith that death was not the end, while I was experiencing the dark night of the soul. As one Anglican priest, Father D. said: 'Life is so transient, it is just a stage and an exercise in survival. The good bits come later.'

I find life quite delightful sometimes, and I would not go along with that, although I can see his point. If the carer and her charge find the subject too difficult to broach, therefore, could the priest act as an intermediary and help them to open up? 'It depends if the priest has a good relationship with the person who is dying,' said Father D. 'If he is a good parish priest with a good relationship, there can be complete honesty. I have discussed the funeral service, even which hymns were to be sung, with the dying person. Another woman who was terminally ill said to me "Father, I'm dying," and I said "Yes, but that's all right." She knew and she was not afraid. It was almost as if she were in a large waiting-room and there was no stress any more. At the other extreme, I have been in a situation where the person involved was scared stiff.'

He believes that the role of the parish priest is to prepare people for a good death, to help the dying look at the positive aspects of the event. 'There are a few people who want the elixir of life, they just don't want to die. Very often, they have no faith, no thesis for living. They are just hanging on, unprepared for the next step.'

In my experience, many elderly people tend to be much more prepared for death than we are; they seem to view it philosophically as the next step. I have heard them say 'I've had a good life.' My mother said, 'I've lived too long', and so did the old man of whom Wendy Saunders spoke: 'I'm surrounded by people who don't make sense,' he told her. 'The days are too long and I don't know what to do with them.'

It is often the carer who shrinks away, as I did, from all thought or mention of death. 'Why is it such an unsociable subject?' asked Jenny Symons. 'There was a time when politics, religion and sex were never discussed in polite society. Now the subject that invites an embarrassed response, a subject that was discussed quite openly until a hundred years ago, is death.'

Some of the embarrassment, she said, had to do with the fact that we do not have the extended family living with us. Death is, therefore, something we do not experience at first hand. 'Parents tell their children that "grandad has gone away"', said Father D. 'That's wrong. They should say, quite simply, "Your granddad is dead."' He described a husband and wife who had suffered 'tremendous pain' for a long time because both were aware of the imminent death of the husband and could not speak about it. He encouraged them and it brought a great release, a preparation for 'a good death'.

On the other side of the coin, there are those who, I felt, went a bit too far, like the carer who startled me when she described how she and her mother – 'two very down-to-earth people from the Midlands' – discussed her mother's death and funeral. 'We began these discussions when my mother was sixty-five,' she told me, 'and we started to put money away to pay for her funeral. You have to face up to it, we all pass through this world. After that, you can relax. I think that's what kept me going, afterwards. I didn't want to be a parasite. It's bad enough to go through a death without worrying how you are going to pay for the funeral. The person should make their will, too. It helps the carer left behind. So many are left alone to deal with a bereavement.'

No elderly person need have sleepless nights worrying who is going to pay for the funeral. Nevertheless, many get very anxious and dread the idea of a 'pauper's funeral'. In reality, it is quite different from its image, said Father D. 'You get the coffin, the service, everything,' he jokes, 'so you can spend your savings with tranquillity.' But, he added, the carer should be aware of the dying person's wishes; for example, does he want to be cremated? 'It's important to know these things.' It is often easier to assume that we know what someone wants, much less painful to assume than to take the trouble to listen to what is said, and to share the thoughts and feelings of that other person about the ending of life.

I have often told myself that I avoided the subject because I did not want to upset or depress my mother. But I know that it was in fact to protect myself – because I did not want to acknowledge the truth, or come to terms with my own emotions. Brushing it under the carpet does not make it go away and there were many signs that the approaching crisis was taking its toll both on her and on me.

When people are ill and frail, the only thing to keep them going is hope that there will be improvement. When they have an inkling that this will not be the case, it is surely understandable if they give up, sometimes, and lapse into depression and apathy. At times like these, it can be helpful for the older person to know that she is not alone, that someone else shares these feelings and understands them.

There are some elderly people, of course, who have the capacity to look upon themselves as apparently immortal. This has a lot to do with the blessing of good health. Wendy Saunders delights in the behaviour of a friend's mother and uncle, aged seventy-eight and eight-four respectively, who plan their next trip abroad and use phrases like 'Next year we'll be doing so and so.' 'The successfully cared for,' Gemma wrote to me, 'are those who feel as if they have something to go on living for. Those who are involved in grandchildren or something like that.' I noticed it in my mother: she came alive when she was with her grandchildren and though she laughed infrequently, she couldn't resist the youngest, Lucy, who is something of a comedian.

As Angela told me: 'One feature I noticed with my mother and which can be easily overlooked is how she lit up when her teenage grandchildren visited. The idea that the frail should be sheltered from the exuberance of youth is sometimes heard. The action seems totally mistaken to me: the capacity of young people to enjoy life without worrying about trivia such as mortgages and clean kitchens may make their interests closer to those of old people than the preoccupations of middle-aged sons and daughters.'

Curiously, too, these younger relatives often seem to have a similar attitude in their carelessness about possessions. How many elderly people nearing the end of their lives begin to give away their things with a carefree abandon, and how many fifty-ish sons and daughters protest: 'Oh, but you shouldn't – you might need it.'

One thing that an elderly person will cling to, and one that can give an enormous amount of affectionate comfort and help sustain an interest in life, is a pet. Research has shown that owning a pet can help people to recover from serious illnesses and can even save lives; more pet owners recover from heart attacks, for instance, than people without pets. It is a consideration that everyone should bear in mind when visiting prospective residential homes: if their charge has a pet, would he or she be allowed to keep it? One carer who wrote to me told how her aunt, a cat lover, would not have dreamt of going anywhere unless her pet could go with her. Some homes allow this, but others forbid animals of any kind.

A national organization called 'Pat Dog' was set up because of the benefit the elderly seem to derive from patting a friendly dog. Hunter is a gentle, golden-haired retriever who regularly visits the Halsford park nursing home in East Grinstead, to warm the hearts of everyone there. All the dogs in this scheme have to pass temperament tests to qualify and are examined by experts for their friendliness and ability to get on with strangers.

It is natural to be anxious about someone who is frail and ill but even if the situation is deteriorating, it is important not to become over-protective. This is a problem not only at home, but in residential homes, too, where professional carers want to feel they are doing the job 'properly': there is a risk that their charges will become institutionalized and apathetic. Given the choice, which many of them are not, there are several old people who would prefer to do things for themselves – 'live' rather than simply vegetate. But if, as sometimes happens, an elderly person has an accident, the carer tends to blame herself. I know I did after my mother had a fall.

Katherine described to me the rage she flew into with her mother who, not wanting to wait until her daughter was free to help, tried to lift a heavy electric fire across a room. 'I was not really angry,' Katherine explained, 'but I burst out because I was terrified of what might have happened, and also felt guilty because I had not gone to help.'

While trying to avoid unnecessary restrictions, there is a

nice balance to be struck between that and risking a careless accident. Accidents can be reduced by taking a few sensible precautions, such as making sure there is an automatic cut-out on electric kettles, that floors are wiped over the moment any liquid is spilled so that there aren't any falls, that ashtrays are conspicuously supplied in the rooms of those who smoke. It is also vital to keep alive freedom of choice, as Joan Welch pointed out. The carers she knows who 'take over' so that their charges are not allowed to choose what they will eat, what they will wear, are mistaken even though well-intentioned. A woman may be confined to a wheelchair but she is still capable of choosing a new dress – indeed, it is a wonderful boost to the morale of any female to do so. I found a friendly store which did not usually exchange goods but which allowed me to buy 'on spec'. That meant that I took home several alternatives for my mother to try on and from which to choose which one she liked. She enjoyed this right to the end. Similarly, there are ways round allowing someone to choose what she would like to read, such as checking whether there is a mobile library in the area. Fundamentally, the elderly person needs to stay as involved as possible and be allowed to make decisions about the various aspects of her life. This commitment to staying alive in small ways as well as large, is in my opinion, very important.

The 'while there's life there's hope' atmosphere created for the cared for can only affect the carer positively. She cannot afford to let herself become discouraged, locked in the moment so that she never thinks of her life ahead. Gretel told me that she had always kept this firmly in mind, and even when her mother was very ill, she refused to give up running her business to be at home all the time. She felt this might have appeared rather callous to the onlooker. 'I don't think I was any the less caring,' she said. 'I knew that, by not having married, I had made certain choices. It was vital to have something of my own after she had gone.'

Others haven't the resources, courage or even physical energy to take this time to be themselves. It is encouraging to know that there are several schemes which could be of use. Some were featured in an impressive and touching video film called *Time to be Me* which was made in the Seaford area, where Graham Millet is a pioneer in the carers' group movement. It is about those who live with and support heavily dependent people at home. For the majority, this takes up most of their life. They come from a variety of backgrounds and from different parts of the country, caring for people with a range of handicaps. But if the problems differ, the carers all experience similar types of demands, frustration and satisfaction, too. They all face a 'life of enormous stress'. The film shows outside help which might be had, such as a home aide service offering long or short periods of domiciliary help to relieve carers, and the Crossroads Care Attendant Scheme in Southend which gives relief to the carer, regularly or spasmodically, for several hours or several days, providing a service in the home to take the strain off the carer.

I used to feel sometimes as if there were a black cloud hanging over the flat and though I strove against it, it was hard not to be influenced by it. But it is understandable if elderly people get depressed. Growing older is depressing in itself, and events or developments in their lives may drag them down further. Isolation, for instance, and seeing their home going downhill because they have neither the money nor energy to do anything about it. When he cannot do as he once did, when he is often in pain, even the most optimistic person is likely to feel depressed.

If you are old it seems as if 'everyone is dying around you' and this hits you, both directly and indirectly – for it is at the same time both a personal loss and also the tolling of your own death knell. Nor is it uplifting to have to depend on other people, particularly if you were once an independent sort of person, surrounded by children and other relatives who all relied on *you*. Again, there is the sense of a double loss: the loss of dependence, and the dependence of others on you being replaced by your dependence on them. When you look at the whole situation, it is surprising that elderly people are not depressed more often.

It is useless to tell your charge to 'pull himself together' or 'think how lucky he is'. Instead, you should accept it as natural that he or she will be 'down' sometimes. You can try to help lift the depression by encouraging your charge to talk, and to listen, by giving him 'permission' to tell all – fears of death, of being dependent, or whatever it is that is getting him down. Above all, you should agree that it is reasonable to feel that way and not a signal of mental illness – for many people fear depression because they think they might be going mad.

People sometimes assume that depression in the elderly is 'just' a sign of getting old, said Dr T. But it is very real and upsetting, both for the sufferers and those around them. He described the case of a woman who telephoned him to say, 'Mother's not well. She's taken to her bed and says she doesn't want to get up.' When Dr T. called, the elderly lady in her seventies said little, and her 'story' was told by her daughter. She said that she managed to get the woman up but no sooner was she dressed then she wanted to go back to bed. As Dr T. had half expected, an examination revealed nothing abnormal about the woman, but afterwards she rolled up and turned herself to the wall. 'There is an expression "to turn your face to the wall",' said Dr T. 'It is often a sign of hopelessness and depression.'

This elderly lady's depression had come on gradually so that the change in mood had been hardly noticeable from one week to the next. Her sense of loss about her life had been extended to a loss of caring about anything, even her nearest and dearest. The family had not suspected depression but simply thought she was being difficult, so the relationship had gone from bad to worse, with a lack of sympathy to add to the troubles. Dr T. started her on a nightly dose of anti-depressant drugs and, eventually, as he said: 'She stopped wanting to hide away in bed and began to communicate again.'

Obviously, these drugs have their place, but I think anyone who reads this book will guess my attitude towards resorting to them as the real solution. They may mask or delay the depression or the anxieties but can never reach the root of what is causing these reactions: the fact that with passing time, all the comforting certainties of youth go. I can empathize with this feeling for, particularly over the past year, I have experienced a deep sense of uncertainty myself. I am not yet even middle-aged but I realize, already, how the things that one took for granted often do not, after all, occur. As you get older, this feeling is exacerbated, until the *only* certainty seems to be death.

It is easy for doctors to dismiss 'anxiety pains and aches' as 'all in the mind'. Maybe they are; but how real they can be. The answer is not a tranquillizer but a listening ear to confirm that the anxiety is appreciated and that the causes can be dealt with. Discussion and psychological support, in my opinion, are far better than drugging someone out of their mind. I don't want to sound too pessimistic, but it is also a fact that the growing depression and anxiety of the later years make suicide much more common, particularly in older men. I was interested to read Dr Lake's compassionate analysis of why such people take their lives. He divides suicides into two groups. In 'anger suicides', the person has chosen the only way they seem to have left to show others just how much rage was there. The message left behind reads: those who ought to care will never understand, but I can make them see a part of what they have done to me; I can make them suffer, too. The survivors, says Dr Lake, must come face to face with the realization that the loss is not just the death itself, but the relationship with the person who died.

He defines the second kind of suicide as the 'fear suicide', which occurs when people haven't the courage to go on with the pain and hopelessness of life. Their anxious fear of living is as great as their fear of death. In this case, those who are being left behind are told that they will be better off without the person who dies – they will be released from having to care, just as the victim will be released from care. Inevitably, those left behind will suffer guilt, or at least regret that they did not understand better what was going through the mind of the person who took his own life.

There is a sense of semi-suicide about those elderly people who start to neglect themselves. They don't seem to care – either for themselves or the impression they are making on the rest of the world. Turning their faces to the wall, as it were, they become dirty and unkempt, in their dress, housekeeping, personal cleanliness, or in all three. They continue to live, but there is a general apathy about them and their appearance which can only affect badly those who live with them.

Helen feels defeated by the dirt and mess in the house. She feels the slovenly atmosphere is creeping under her skin and makes halfhearted attempts to do something about it when her mother has gone to bed. Her health is now suffering because she has developed a cancer phobia. 'My life is a nightmare of looking for lumps or bleeding, partly due to my mother's last two operations being for cancer. She is remarkably brave and stoical sort of person and seems to have convinced herself she is cured, despite six-monthly check-ups. As she takes this attitude, how can I complain or whine?'

Helen complained to me, however, that no one has spoken to her honestly about her mother's condition. 'I have to assume it is likely to break out again somewhere else, but at her age they are hoping for 'natural causes' to intervene first. For both our sakes, I hope so, too. What I've seen of cancer treatment, both physical and mental, has destroyed a lot of my faith in doctors.'

Everyone has their own idea of whether or not people should be told if their illness is terminal. Professional people differ very much in their views, which will sometimes clash with those of the carer. In my own case, my father was told he had cancer, although we were of the opinion that it would have been better for him if he had not known. Once it was confirmed, he gave up and would not eat.

Father D., who has worked in several hospices for the dying, said he had noted the different ways in which people react when they know they are going to die. 'There have been those who booked to go on a world cruise, the day they were told, others whose minds have just gone a blank and others who go into a flat spin and just don't know how to cope. Personally, I don't think I would like to be told the exact time of my death. I'd rather soldier on and take more tablets. But that is my view.'

There are some people who can cope better by not knowing. There are others who 'know' without being told. According to Jenny Symons: 'Be prepared when they want to talk about it. The need comes and goes and you have to allow them that, but don't push it. There is an uncertain period when they might recover or not, so you must strike a balance between not hitting them in the face with the fact they are going to die, nor totally denying it. If you collude by ignoring it, you prevent them talking about it which may be something you will bitterly regret.'

An Open University course on the care of the elderly contains some excellent case history studies, such as that of Mrs Vidgeon who describes how she faced up to her husband's terminal cancer and death. She tells how, after the doctor had advised her to try to break the news, she walked home with her mind a total blank. Her first reaction was fear of being alone and unable to cope. But her husband met her halfway by saying: 'Well, it's cancer, isn't it?'

The months passed and she was saddened by the deterioration in his health. He had always been a keen gardener; now she had 'literally to lean him against the coal bunker' so that he might watch while she tended the garden. Mrs Vidgeon found that the 'appalling thing' was the disappearance of all the things they had done together . . . 'This was the time of grief, not afterwards, because you knew he was at peace.'

Dr Lake has pointed out that when you know in advance that somebody is going to die, it can help make the work of grieving an enriching experience. But if carers are nervous about discussing the subject, or unsure how to treat a dying resident, this may inhibit those who are in their care from being able to express mourning, or their fears about dying. Spiritual help is a basic need but staff in terminal care homes may not offer it if they feel it is likely to be rejected.

Father D., who has worked at the St Christopher hospice in London and has recently joined one in Chichester says that he finds it 'a tremendous privilege to help someone to die well – there is something almost sacramental about it'. Yet there are establishments where those who want to practise their religion are met with practical difficulties, lack of understanding of their needs, sometimes even ridicule. There is currently a serious lack of support in many homes to help staff with training advice, information and counselling in handling some of the social problems connected with terminal care. A recent draft from the DHSS, 'Residential Homes for the Elderly', has stated that wherever possible, a dying resident in such homes should not be moved to a special room, nor be transferred to hospital. Caring for dying residents may place an extra strain on staff but the head of the home should be encouraged to call on the primary health care services for help. Where a relative wishes to help in nursing a sick or dying relative, the home should welcome and encourage such involvement.

Again, it depends on the individual carer as to whether she can cope with this. Zena could not imagine doing anything but staying at the hospital during her mother's last hours. Helen drove to her business just hours before her mother died, and left nurses to cope. Anna came away from the hospital because she felt, 'I couldn't do any more. I felt exhausted.' The connotations of a relative being admitted to a hospice are sometimes more than the carer can take. It will be their breaking point.

Jonathan talked to me a few months ago about his wife, who has cancer. 'She's a little angel one moment, a little devil the next – it's the illness that makes them like that.' He was already grieving for the wife he knew; nevertheless, he was still in control of the situation. His wife was with him, at home, and there was the daily routine of caring, medication, and doctor's visits. Recently, when she was admitted to a home for terminal care, he broke down. Cancer had become almost a way of life and he had learned to cope with it. Now he was having to face death.

Dying is a continuous process. It is not an isolated event divorced from life but the obverse side of the coin and, as such, ever encroaching. It should be natural, therefore, when we speak of the 'quality of life' that we include the 'quality of dying' too. According to the Voluntary Euthanasia Society, 'There is a strong case based on common sense and compassion for granting the wish of terminal patients for a merciful release from prolonged and useless suffering.'

In writing this, I take a deep breath and pause, for I am aware that if 'cancer' is a highly emotive word for many people, with its accompanying images of fear, then for them 'euthanasia' may be unmentionable. We all hope that when the time comes we shall die peacefully, with dignity and without prolonged suffering. Yet there are many who must still endure a long-drawn-out and disturbing process of degeneration, the misery of which cannot always be relieved by pain killers and sedatives.

Father D. echoes much of the Church's opinion in his adamant statement: 'It is ethically wrong and against Christian teaching to ask someone to help you die. If you are going to do it, you must take the initiative yourself. I have seen people, when faced with death, say, 'No, I'm not ready yet.' He said that some people did not approve of the hospice movement because very strong drugs were given which might accelerate death. 'The important thing is that people have the right to die with dignity and without pain.'

While the Voluntary Euthanasia Society agrees that the best possible nursing is available through the hospice movement for those who need and want such care, even so, some patients obtain inadequate relief from pain and distress. 'Breathlessness, difficulties in swallowing, bed sores, incontinence and other miseries can all be ameliorated by devoted nursing but this will not satisfy the patient who wants a clean death. The patient who continually needs another person to wipe his nose, stop his tongue from hanging out or change his sheets may find it more dignified to opt for death.' Even if every patient could be cared for in a hospice, it underlines, there would still be the need for voluntary euthanasia. 'Not everyone wants to spend his last weeks, months, or even years in an institution, however benevolent; many want to die at home.'

The case for voluntary euthanasia has been well stated by the prominent Methodist, the late Rev. Leslie Weatherhead: 'I sincerely believe that those who come after us will wonder why on earth we kept a human being alive against his own will when all the dignity, meaning and beauty of life has vanished . . . when any gain to anyone was clearly impossible, and when we should have been punished by the state if we kept an animal alive in similar physical conditions.'

Many people, myself included, shy away from any thought of euthanasia, coupling it possibly with a sort of 1984-ish attitude toward the elderly, infirm and unwanted. It is a topic which comes under fire in any debate. The history of the Voluntary Euthanasia Society, however, marks a changing climate of opinion since its inception in 1935. Public disquiet about the problems of dying and the need to make the act more gentle has continued to grow since then. It led to the enactment of the Suicide Act without opposition in 1961, making it no longer a criminal offence to commit suicide or to attempt to do so. But it left both doctor and patient in a difficult position, since the Act provided that if a doctor carried out his patient's wishes to release him from his suffering, he risked prosecution. In September 1976, a national opinion poll found that 69 per cent agreed that 'the law should allow adults to receive medical help to an immediate peaceful death, if suffering from incurable illness that is intolerable to them, provided they have previously requested such help in writing'. A second question which asked the same people whether they had known someone who had suffered within the previous five years from such an illness was confirmed by 37 per cent, thus emphasizing the reality of the problem.

In November 1978, another poll asked: 'Do you agree that if a patient is suffering from a distressing and incurable illness, a doctor should be allowed to supply that patient with the means to end his own life, if the patient wishes it?' Although this question was more specifically concerned with suicide, 62 per cent came out in support, with majority support among all religious denominations, except Roman Catholics who were evenly divided.

The Society receives many letters telling of the prolonged pain and considerable distress endured by dying friends and relatives, such as the following:

> My wife aged seventy suffered a massive stroke six years ago, and another stroke two years ago. She has now lost all balance control, is incontinent, unable to move without help and suffers frequent petit mal epileptic seizures. A recent neurological evaluation revealed continuing irreversible degeneration of the central nervous system. She suffers excruciating pain which the strongest medication only temporarily moderates. She just lies in bed, staring at the ceiling, praying to die. All her days are spent in agonizing over the hopelessness of her plight, her terrible pain, the bitter uselessness of her life and her inability to die.

Another woman wrote: 'I am interested in voluntary euthanasia as for the last year I have watched my dear mother dying of cancer. I visit her, every night, and it is hell for me to see her in pain and fading away. I cannot understand why people are allowed to linger like this. She has prayed to die. I should hate to cause anyone the pain I have endured, watching her.'

'We are practising Christians over many years,' writes a man. 'I am seventy-seven and my wife seventy-three. We have discussed voluntary euthanasia with our two married daughters and we agree that if ever we came to suffer from a terminal illness we do not want to be subjected to any prolonged survival treatment, not only for our sakes but for theirs.'

I know that this dilemma is something that faces many carers, some who are religiously deeply committed. There are those who say 'It's not natural.' But human ageing is not 'natural'; it is to an extent 'man made' by our sentimentalism and medical advances. I read with interest the following comment of one writer:

> Most creatures out in the wilderness die off or are killed off at the first loss of physical or mental power. In a sense, ageing, real ageing, the continuation of living through the whole long period of sensescence, is a human invention and perhaps a relatively recent one at that. Our remote ancestors probably looked after their aged relatives much in the fashion of some aboriginal cultures, by one or another form of that euphemism, euthanasia.

There are now twenty-seven societies united in the World Federation of Right to Die Societies. In Holland, active voluntary euthanasia is already practised in certain hospitals, apparently within the law.

In Britain, it is possible to protect oneself against unwanted medical survival by signing the Voluntary Euthanasia Society's advance declaration or 'Living Will', which is then lodged with one's doctor as an indication of one's wishes, should the time come when it is no longer possible to take part in decisions about one's future. The Voluntary Euthanasia Society's advice in addition is to consider appointing a special Power of Attorney in favour of one or two trusted people, empowering them to deal with doctors, nurses, hospitals, and even relations, to ensure that treatment is not given contrary to the wishes expressed in the declaration.

My mother's death was peaceful – she went to sleep in my arms. I had heard the phrase 'died peacefully in her sleep' many times, but never really believed it before. But death is painful for those who must watch it, must lose their beloved. I asked Father D. to give some advice for those who are aware that soon they must face it and have doubts about whether they are able to. 'Ask the doctor what it is like to see a death,' he said. 'Learn about it, simple things like keeping the window a little open and the lips moist. Never talk as if they are gone because they can hear you. If he is a caring doctor, he can tell you these things. There are simple points you can learn and which will help you, so do get some advice.'

He is anxious, however, about those who have just been bereaved being exploited by funeral directors. 'You are in a state of shock when you telephone them and they know you are unlikely to quibble over the price. But you should steel yourself to "shop around" a bit. I am convinced that if people did that the prices would come down.'

Mrs Vidgeon described her immediate reaction on her husband's death: 'There was no feeling. You can't explain it. It was nothing to do with me. I said to my son, "We must go home." I longed to be home.' They sat down and talked about the things that they had to do and she felt very afraid that she would not be able to cope, she would be frightened of living alone. 'But I knew I had to face it and so I started – living alone.'

Said Caroline: 'As a carer you just have to be there and then chucked back into the world to start all over again when the crisis is over. That's not easy.'

7. Picking up the Pieces

You are alone. If you have been a single daughter carer, you are probably facing being on your own for the first time in your life, separated from the person you have known since you were a small child. Comparisons are difficult to make when considering the impact of bereavement – each is unique just as each relationship was unique. The grief of a daughter who has looked after a mother or father has a special quality about it. She has invested a large part of her life in the caring of her parent and in doing so, has not gone through the process of creating a family life of her own. Her solitude is, therefore, mixed with a sometime sense of bitterness: 'I have given my life to this and now my purpose has gone.' The single daughter has missed out but, at the same time, because she has apparently 'chosen' to stay at home, other people may find it more difficult to sympathize with her, as they would with, say, someone who has lost a husband or wife.

As Zena told me: 'People talk about how devastating it is to lose a husband or wife but I have known my parents for nearly fifty years. That's a lifetime.'

Overnight, all that has been swept away and you are faced, in mid-life, with the prospect of having to assert your individuality, maybe establish your own identity for the first time. It is a daunting prospect.

At the beginning, however, you probably cannot even realize what is involved. You, the carer, need care during those first raw hours and days. With any luck you will be whisked away, as I was, to stay with caring relatives and not have to return home to be alone. But thought should be given to them, too. They may feel they must submerge their own grief, at least at first, in caring for you, but they have a right to their emotions, too. A friend of mine, bound up in the grief of having lost his wife, suddenly, in the middle of the night, turned to his son, realizing that he had lost his mother, too. In Mrs Vidgeon's case, no one seemed to care about her son and his personal sorrow for his father; he had to be his mother's entire consolation. She shut herself up in her bedroom and left him to await the hearse. 'And off we went,' she said, 'and it was nothing to do with me.'

I know that feeling. I have been through it twice. It seems as if you are in a dream from which surely you will awaken to find that everything is as it was. This trance-like state usually carries you through the days which lead to the funeral, and meanwhile there are things to be done. One purpose of ritual is to carry people through emotional occasions in a prescribed way so that they do not need to think it out, only follow it through. The fact that you *have* to do these things can be a saving grace and there is much professional opinion to confirm that we should perform them, ourselves, if at all possible, and not be tempted to let someone take over for us.

Throughout those days, I cried a lot. I cannot remember very much except my continual dissolving into tears until my face was swollen beyond recognition. I was offered various tablets, but I stuck to my beliefs about sedation and took sleeping pills on only the first two nights. I also wanted to experience my grief; I knew I couldn't take tranquillizers forever and that, sooner or later, it would overwhelm me. So I cried. People react to death in different ways. Some carers have described to me the overwhelming rage they have felt as they experience the abortive quality of their lives: 'I've given her (or him) everything and now this – and what am *I* going to do?' As I explained in the previous chapter, I seemed to have purged myself of anger during the grieving process that began while my mother was still alive. My sister felt completely stunned, and when she continued to be apparently calm and collected, became anxious that there must be 'something wrong' because she couldn't let go as I did. That was to come later. Each of us has our own pace. Every emotion is 'permissible' although many bereaved carers have confided to me that they felt they 'ought' to feel only a sense of loss. Guilt, anger, even flashes of humour – all is normal. In my case I howled. I drowned myself in tears and when I came to the surface, eventually, it was to realize that a chapter had closed in my life. I, who had seen myself as every 'child' does, to some degree – an extension of my parent – had lost the sense of my own immortality. But I didn't want the chapter to end like this. I wasn't prepared for it. I didn't want to feel the ground slipping from beneath my feet. I clung to every possession of my mother's. For a long while, the place was a mausoleum of her last shopping lists, a box of biscuits she had been given at Christmas; her toothbrush stayed in the bathroom rack. I have recognized this feeling in some of the carers' homes I have visited. It seems as if time is suspended, as if the person has just gone out for a while and will return.

'Displays of grief in Britain, unlike Eastern nations, are regarded as over-emotional and bad-mannered,' commented Jenny Symons. 'Some people simply do not know what to do when they see the bereaved person in the street. A few solve the problem by crossing the road and pretending not to see their neighbour or friend. Others try to jolly the mourner out of her grief, hoping to stem the floods of tears with constant reminders that "life goes on".'

Maybe it does. But at this moment it has come to a grinding halt. Jenny's remarks became familiar to my sister and me. At first, certainly, we were inundated with sympathy; then, when we showed no signs of 'pulling ourselves together' or agreeing with them that it was 'all for the best' (the best for who?), we watched the embarrassment grow before people started to avoid us. We became sensitive to the reactions of others faced by parental bereavement around that time; almost as if, by comparison, we were trying to convince ourselves that our behaviour was 'normal'. One woman's reaction gave us the biggest laugh we had had in months, although the humour might be somewhat black.

On hearing of her father's death, she dumped her children and hurried to his home. She was gone a week. My sister prepared herself with tea and sympathy for her return. She was startled, therefore, when all Irene could talk about was a splendid garden shed in her parents' garden. If the house were put up for sale, as it probably would be, could they remove it? She really could do with this shed because their own was so dilapidated. To be charitable, we agreed that it must be a case of delayed shock and watched her for a week or two for signs of her breaking down. Not a bit of it! It was definitely the fate of that shed which worried her much more than her father's death.

At the other extreme, a letter in a national magazine, appealing for carers to contact me for this book brought forth a poignant letter from a friend whom we had not seen for years. She wrote: 'I miss my Ma so much and it is just coming up to the first anniversary, which I'm dreading. I've spent this last year trying, without much success, to rebuild my life, as I nursed her right to the end, single-handed.' We decided that, if in future, we heard of a friend bereaved of a parent, we would make a point of keeping in contact and giving support, for months after the death rather than days or weeks. We would not, as we found most people did, 'drop the subject' when it was thought to be 'time' to be over it.

On this point I had to disagree with Father D., who, when describing a parisioner who had continued to mourn her husband, said that a year after his death she was still 'determined not to get over it'. Willpower does not come into it, as a friend of mine commented on the inconsolable loss of his wife. Whatever commonsense tells you should do, your emotions are wayward beyond conscious control. 'You never get over it,' said this friend, 'but you learn to live with it.'

I can only attribute Father D.'s attitude to his wonderful faith that 'the good bits are to come'. In African society, he pointed out, they have to earn a living so they have one big 'do' and then get on with life. We keep it all suppressed, he said: 'We have the funeral and then keep on mourning.'

With the best will in the world, we could not behave like his

Africans. At the time of writing, it is over a year since my mother died, and like many former carers I have met, we have our 'good' days and our 'bad' ones. You cannot throw away so many years as easily as that! I am inclined to agree with Jenny Symons who said that it takes a good two years to get over a close bereavement, and 'for some people the time can be much longer'. Jenny has suffered her own close loss, the death of a son.

She said: 'You think that something like that only happens to other people. Then the realization of what has happened to you sets in. You feel devastated, you can't possibly survive it. You cannot visualize life will ever be happy or normal again. The first year is the worst. You keep thinking back to 'this time last year'. After the first anniversary it does get easier, but there is still a lot of emptiness in life.'

Anna understands this feeling. 'Sometimes I wake up in the mornings and think 'What am I living for?' she admitted. 'I don't feel I can pick up the pieces. I lost so many years but there was no one else to do it. And now that it's all over no one cares what happens to me!'

The personal column of the National Council for Carers and their Elderly Dependants tells many a tale of the difficulties of parental bereavement, when you read between the lines: 'Recently bereaved carer would like to contact another for mutual caring relationship.' (Often, says Jenny Symons, a carer needs to continue by going into another caring situation.); 'Fifty-year-old lady ex-carer who has difficulty in facing life after a recent bereavement would like to hear from a person in a similiar position', runs another.

An essential part of the Council's work is to try to provide companionship for these former carers. Many feel that their job is done when their charge has died but the carers' groups appreciate that their invaluable experience in caring can be a strength and support to those who are still suffering their loss. Some people have smoother passages through bereavement than others, some seem to be doing excellently and then slip back but, as Jenny insists, as time goes by the sharper pain of grief will fade, although the memories remain.

Sometimes, in a society which expects a stiff upper lip, people do not go through all the processes of grieving, nor complete them satisfactorily. There is a great deal of violent emotion being worked out, particularly where one person has had their life disrupted or restricted because of the need to care for someone else. They need to face up to these emotions, however alien they might seem to the business of grieving, they need to realize that they are not 'nasty' because they feel these unacceptable reactions, and accept that it is all part of a complex relationship. Unless it is completed, they cannot go on to restructure their lives. Cruse does excellent work with its counselling, giving 'permission to grieve'. The people who work for it are compassionate and caring; many of them have been through a bereavement themselves. I have been helped by a lovely lady whom I know only by her Christian name, Joan, and who suffered the loss of a dear husband. More often than not, she does no more than listen to my outpourings, but that is vitally necessary and there are so many people who have no one to tell.

'Working for Cruse can be emotionally draining,' said Jenny Symons. 'Most counsellors can do only three or four years before they need a break. You have to learn to cope with people's sadness and tears. We all get involved to some extent, but if you are going to give comfort, you have to remain a little bit detached.' Although Cruse was originally founded to help those who had lost husbands, counselling has now been extended to anyone who is bereaved – from people who have lost parents to anyone who has lived with someone else and lost them, including gay couples.

To grieve for a parent is, according to Dr Lake, often harder than any other kind of grieving. We may have known our parents longer than anyone else but that is not to say we know them well, he suggests. The reasons for this are various: they belong to a different generation; maybe their own parents did not encourage a relaxed atmosphere;

or they have held on to the power that parenthood gives. It could also be that it is the fault of the 'children', who are hesitant in viewing them as anything other than parents. My sister is trying to establish a situation of equality and friendship with her children now, telling them about things she did when she was a child, putting herself in their position when they come to her for advice. She is hopeful that they will grow up to see her as a 'person in her own right' and not just 'Mum'.

Dr Lake points out that grieving is difficult to initiate when we have felt anger toward the parent, or been forced to do what he or she wanted when this conflicted with our own wishes. 'We are taught that love is natural between child and parent,' he writes, 'and we feel there is something unnatural if we do not love ours. It is, says society, our duty to love them.'

I have heard of this ambivalence from several of the carers who contacted me. It might not have been expressed openly, but there was a sense of mixed emotions about the death. Perhaps they feared they would shock me if they had come right out and said, 'Yes, in some ways I'm glad my parent has died and my caring days are over.' They were freed to make what they could out of the rest of their lives. I can understand these feelings. I can remember my own fury at being forced into a role which I realized was not natural to me, at the sense of my life going by and the frustration of not being able to do what I wanted. I remember my first meeting with the vivacious P.M. It was at a NCCED twenty-first anniversary celebration, when she made an instant impression as she made her entrance dressed from top to toe in vibrant blue.

'I feel wonderful,' she exclaimed. 'I'm being me for the first time in my life and it's a lovely feeling.'

Obviously, there was a certain amount of bravado in her words, for I have since come to know her as a gentle and caring woman who has taken on other caring situations since the death of her mother. She loved and misses the elderly woman but she had the honesty to break that taboo which keeps many people from speaking openly about their real feelings. If only they could do so, they would be free to mourn more genuinely. Dr Lake has written that his overall impression is that many people never grieve fully for the loss of the real people their parents were, simply because of this embargo.

For P.M., in the midst of her grief, there was an element of relief about the death of her mother and she had the courage to admit it. It set her free to do the travelling she adores which is what she intends to do for as long as she can. Anna's relief came about not only because somebody whom she loved very much and whose life had lost its quality was released from pain, but also because her own life time of being 'put down' was over.

Anna, today, is angry although it is suppressed. But every now and again you sense it bubbling up and ready to over-spill. 'When my father died, we were left in chaos because there was no will,' she said. 'I have never been myself, always in some kind of enslavement. When I write to people now, my letters are such a mixture of emotions. I am happy and sad at the same time. I've come to the end of years and years of it. I really don't know what I feel at the moment. I just live from day to day. I get up in the morning, make myself a cup of tea and do the crossword. I go to the market like the French, shopping for what I need, every day. I don't always cook, just have a cheese sandwich. I can't think about the future – I don't feel at the moment there is one for me. I'm just trying to de-stress myself. When I look back, I've been under severe stress for ten years.'

I don't want to sound too hard on Father D., who is a pleasant enough person, but I sometimes find his attitudes difficult to understand. 'I think you should care for the carers,' he agreed. 'But you mustn't give them too much sympathy or they are going to need more. If you don't keep on about how marvellous they've been, they won't feel so hardly done by. Just say "You did a good job but now it's over, what are you going to do?" That way you're helping them toward living a normal life.'

In my own experience, and from speaking with many other carers, I know it is not as simple as that: society doesn't really want to listen. P.M. however is an exception who shares his view. She said that she has become 'rather blasé about death in the family'. Her surviving relatives are very elderly, two aunts, one of eighty-one caring for the other of eighty-nine. P.M. is concerned for them but philosophical about enjoying her life now. Speaking of a forthcoming trip to the States when she must leave them for some time, she said: 'I'll break the news to them over a bottle of champagne.'

We talked in the attractive flat I have described earlier with its splendid view over the sea. Although her mother disliked it, P.M. loves her home and will continue to use it as a base for her travels. By no means wealthy, she can nevertheless afford to stay where she is. But the question of housing can become a serious issue to single daughters left behind with a sudden reduction in finances, as Heather McKenzie has pointed out. Money soon rears its ugly head.

Perhaps I was particularly sensitive, but I found it up-setting that bills required to be paid so urgently, within days of my mother's death, while such things as the death grant, even an outstanding pension payment, were much more tardy. For several reasons, I moved within months of her death, which went against the advice I have had from several experts. Father D. said: 'Don't move, that's what I advise. Stay where you are and get used to being by yourself. If you sell up and go somewhere new, you begin to look around and think "Where has my home gone?"'

It is a very personal choice – staying or going. A friend of mine has found enormous comfort in staying on in the house he shared with his wife for a number of years – a house that she loved and made into a beautiful home.

It is true, sometimes, that the psychological upheaval can be more disturbing than the physical one. I know I had terrible pangs of regret on the eve of my own removal. But, some months later, I can say I feel this initial move was positive. I know I shall not stay in my present home for ever but the step was right. Our flat held bad memories for both of us and it had been my mother's ambition to get out of it. As someone said to me, 'It's not bricks and mortar but one's personal possessions which hold the memories.'

Other carers have felt it was in their better interests to stay where they were. Zena was adamant: 'I don't want to move out of the house. It is my family home. *All* my memories are here. If I didn't have this, what should I have?'

Helen debated the question seriously and decided to stay. Her home is an attractive cottage in the town centre, filled with her mother's possessions, including several pet birds. Helen seems able to deal with it without being over-whelmed. 'We created this home together,' she said. 'After my father died, we moved around the town a lot and then settled here and created it without any menfolk to help. I am fond of this place.'

Anna is also rooted in the flat she shared with her mother. The neighbours have been kind, she says; she would feel a stranger if she moved and had to start again. But I couldn't help getting the impression that she seemed paralyzed by her past 'enslavement' and could not now develop.

Even if they decide to stay put, most carers say they would enjoy a temporary break to reacclimatize themselves. The NCCED has a list of holiday addresses which have been compiled from recommendations in response to their re-quest for holiday suggestions – places where an exhausted person can find peace and quiet, good food, comfort, real relaxation and an opportunity to 're-charge the batteries'. The classic 'getting away from it all, abroad' might be beyond some carers' means. These holidays are positive and inexpensive. A retreat could be another idea, even if one is not particularly religious – it would give one space and time to think.

Joan Welch spends a lot of time in the aftercare of carers and, on several occasions, has acted as a go-between for those who cannot fight for themselves. In her view, there is some shabby treatment of women who are in a bad psychological state, and needy. She described the case of one woman who had looked after her father for five years. She suffered badly from migraine but when the father died and she tried to obtain sick pay, she was told social security would help, only if she obtained a medical certificate. 'That girl's father had just died and the house was falling down around her,' said Joan Welch, 'but the doctor would not give her a certificate. The best thing she could do, he said, was find herself a job.'

Another woman who was ill was given a medical certificate but the social services refused to pay, in this deserving case. Joan Welch took up cudgels on her behalf, and a giro cheque arrived two days later. The problem was that she had the money, on paper – her mother had left her everything – but she could not touch it because, coincidentally, both her solicitor and bank manager were on holiday. 'All that girl was asking for was enough money to keep her head above water until they got back,' said Joan Welch.

Many one-time carers have to learn to live on a smaller budget. A big problem, I found, was trying to deal with financial decisions and continue to earn a living at a period of intense grieving. I think this strikes unmarried 'children' hard. The shock, the numbness, the disbelief that it cannot be happening to you, even though you may have seen it coming for some time, make financial and personal problems doubly hard to bear. Then the dreamlike stage passes and life seems futile, you become nervy and cannot sleep. It seems as if you have no good prospects and your mood swings from depression to anger, back to depression. You resent the rest of the world: those people who have lives of their own.

When I sat, sipping a glass of wine, with Anna in her flat, I said that maybe we could meet up again as we had something in common. I noted an instant switching off and did not pursue this. Later, she told me: 'I've been alone a lot of my life and I don't need to be with just anyone now, so as not to be alone. I choose when I'll see people and, at the moment, I want to stay alone. I'm determined not to take tranquillizers, I don't agree with them. But I wake at three in the morning and feel lost and wonder what will happen to me.'

Sometimes, this edginess is contrasted with a feeling of lethargy. You just can't be bothered to do anything. I remember how I had to push myself to write a commissioned feature, just weeks after my mother's death. Each time I stopped, I felt I couldn't summon enough energy to begin again. Zena identified with this. 'I always used to rush about,' she said, 'but I'm so lazy now. I couldn't wait to finish a meal; now I just sit over it.'

And so the process continues. My sister's grief, held back for so long, expressed itself, as we knew it would, later on. The pieces she had to fit together in her life were of a different nature to mine. The feeling was no less intense but I envied her the automatic everyday caring she had to do for her family. It carried her along, while I seemed to have come to an impasse. The children might sometimes seem an intrusion on her mourning but they were there, they needed her. Overnight, in common with many other single daughter carers, I felt I had been made redundant.

My sister and I shared the experience which is defined as 'searching' – that anxious examination of faces in the street, at social gatherings, coupled sometimes with the shock of seeing an elderly woman who 'looked like her'. Susan admitted that days after the death, while I was staying with her, she had picked up the telephone and dialled the number of the flat. 'I let it ring and ring and ring,' she told me. 'I was convinced that it would be answered. I thought I must be going mad.' She also found herself looking at clothes, in shops, that would be suitable for our mother. Another carer told me that for a long time, whenever the door bell rang she was certain it was her dead father who had once more lost his key.

Said Jenny Symons, 'It is believed that these periods of non-acceptance are nature's way of helping us accept our bereavement gradually. But people don't know about these stages and they feel afraid; they get a lot of comfort when we explain. They realize they are not after all going out of their minds. The natural way of bereavement is to pass through all these stages and emotions, from total depression to furious anger – accept them as you go through them, facing them as you do so. I wait and see what people feel, and try to understand. Then I go along with them, following the way they are taking.'

Grief is at once something we all share and a personal experience in which we feel totally alone. There are aspects of grieving we all have in common, but no two people can ever feel quite the same. Knowing about grief is not the same as knowing grief. One of the frightening aspects of it is that we feel out of control. We believe we're over it and then it breaks through and the wound is opened up again.

Guilt is an inherent emotion that accompanies it. We blame ourselves for 'letting' the person die even though there was all the evidence it was inevitable. We berate ourselves for not doing enough and if that person happened to die while we were not there, we feel guilty again. My sister and I have our individual guilts. As I have said previously, neither of us could bring ourselves to accept the fact she was dying, even though it was more than hinted at by several doctors. I could not stop blaming myself because I did not spend her last night with her at the nursing home. This changed to a rage at the staff that they had not done enough for her, our GP for his, to me, callous attitudes to age. Later on, I was to share this with Andrew who cared for his aunt devotedly as she moved from bewilderment into dementia. He gave up his home to move to the South Coast to be with her, commuting to London, every day. Andrew is a warm hearted and caring person. He is always ready to help any lame dog. No one could have done more than he did. Nevertheless, he was not with his aunt when she died and voiced his anger with the nursing home because it did not make him fully aware of the state of the elderly lady's health during her last hours. This anger can also be directed against the person who died, for having left the carer alone.

'I got so angry with him,' one carer told me, a short while after the death of her father. 'I thought I must be going mad. I used to stomp along the road muttering to myself "How dare you! You've died and so quickly we haven't even been able to discuss what *I* do with *my* life. You've taken all my best years and left me with nothing!"' Another carer told me how he felt furious every time he saw what he considered to be an unChristian and unpleasant neighbour, the same age as his beloved wife who had died in her fifties. Dorothy raged when the 'old people', her elderly in-laws for whom she cares, told her she was 'lucky to have her sons still'. She felt angry because they were still alive and in their nineties while her husband had died in his prime. 'I was so angry that I lost my faith,' she told me. 'Although I had always been a regular churchgoer I raged at God for allowing it to happen. It seemed so unfair.'

Violent or unexpected death can make us feel not only empty and alone but also anxious, as our imaginations work overtime and we think of what he or she might have suffered while we were not there. This can fill us with self-rejection and more guilt; it can depress people to the point of suicide. Heather McKenzie advises that if this type of depression continues or worsens it is important to see a doctor. Although each of us has a different rate of adjusting to normal life, long-term grieving like this suggests we might need medical help.

Generally, most of us eventually arrive at the stage of acceptance and can set about creating a new life. However, Jenny Symons pointed out, it is natural to be flung back to previous stages just when you thought you were 'getting over it'. When there is another, less important loss – the death of a pet cat or dog for instance – this can tilt one over the edge, making one regress to a previous stage. She told the story of one young woman whom she was counselling, who had had quite serious family losses but seemed to have coped stoically. Then her cat was run over and that was the last straw. 'Everything is dying,' she cried. 'I was so strong before. I didn't give in.' Jenny pointed out that as she had not grieved naturally before, she needed to do so now. 'I was, as it were, giving her permission to grieve. She had to let it come out, sooner or later, so that she could begin to live again.'

Just as there must be a grieving period, as Jenny says, there also must come a time when this must be completed. Sometimes people need encouragement to go out into the world again and pick up the threads. For this reason, she is wary of an interest in spiritualism, seeing it pose a danger that the person in question will not come to accept the death: 'They continue to look back, to hold on, and cannot allow themselves to move forward.'

What I found more disturbing were the physical traits of those former carers who seemed to be 'stuck' in their present lives and unable to move on. There was, as I have remarked before, a certain Peter Pan sense about them: Anna, nearly fifty, who talked to me with a baby blue bow in her hair; Miss E., who seemed like an elderly child who had cared for her mother and now appears herself to be 'babied' by the remaining brothers and sisters-in-law. Joyce said to me quite frankly: 'When I moved in with my mother, I reverted to early teenage years. I have been a slow developer and never really found independence until lately. I was in my forties when my father died. Even now, I find it hard to be responsible and to think about material things.' Even the stoical Dorothy says that the 'old people' still see her as a 'young thing', although she is past retirement age.

Out of completed grief will spring a new responsibility for one's own life, if only we can look ahead and not be lost in a mire of regrets for opportunities which have passed us by. It is not always easy to accept that we must say goodbye to a part of our childhood's dependence, to move on into adulthood in our own right. I felt that Zena still had some way to go when she told me: 'I am alone. I've lived with these two people for nearly fifty years and we did everything together. We used to garden together, and when we went shopping, we all went together.'

Zena still seems to be resentful of her parents for having

died and left her alone and, like a child, she also seems determined to 'spite them' by not making any effort to move on. She has withdrawn into herself and lavishes all her affection on her cat. She reminded me of a peevish child. Perhaps, though, it is early days yet.

If you can bring yourself to make the leap, this can be a very creative time for a single person carer. It depends, of course, how she or he decides to live. There is always a choice, and it will probably be between continuing with the role that has been allotted by other members of the family without making any attempt to resist the pressures, or facing up to the people whom you are going to disappoint. Neither is an easy choice – the first way means that you continue to give up the chance of becoming a person in your own right; the second demands a lot of you at a time when your loss is already making you feel vulnerable. One way or the other, the situation forces you to look at your life and your relationships. It would probably suit other people better if you stayed as you were. The present 'you' has been shaped for the role for a long time, by those who are probably stronger than you. According to Dr Lake: 'People will be shocked if you seem to be enjoying life or building a new existence for yourself.'

I think a few were startled by P.M.'s brilliant blue outfit and announcement that she was happy. But grieving must be allowed to include the realization of your own needs: to be independent, and to be rid of other people's interference and opposition. P.M. could have continued to smoulder with the bitterness of wasted years but she decided to behave otherwise, to simply get on with life and forget the time when she was subject to what her mother wanted of her.

Anna seems to be still in thrall to tyranny. 'I have never been allowed to be myself,' she said. 'I wanted to paint and I never have, or not what I wanted to paint. I would also like to have gone in for acting but my parents were so square they wouldn't let me. I am living on a government pension. I don't want to touch my earnings until I reach my sixties. I would like to get a part-time job. I would like to go to the Lake District or to Paris – I would like to travel,' she said, wistfully. I had a feeling she won't. I could not help but make the comparison with P.M., who is some twelve years older.

'How do I travel?' P.M. said. 'I have to draw out my savings. I am always hoping for a premium bond to come up.' She plans to go to China, Australia, New Zealand and back to the USSR. She is fortunate in having a friend who will keep an eye on the flat. Her childlike enthusiasm is of the positive kind.

'So many people plan and worry about their lives and are so terribly solemn,' she said. 'When Mamma went, it was a Friday, there was the funeral the following week, and then I went off to India. It was not successful – perhaps it was too soon – but I'm better now. People say that I look very well, all the strain is gone. I do feel that I am being really me.'

She was honest here in voicing what many carers keep quiet about: however much they love the person they have cared for, they are not able to live their lives to their full extent. P.M. is 'doing something with her life', as she said. 'I never imagined I should do all this travelling. I've been to Russia three times in a year and I love it. I like the people. I went to the Hermitage on my own and did four operas. I intend to do all the long hauls while I still have good health.'

P.M. is not angry or sorry for herself in the way that Anna is. She says she is a survivor. Her present 'survival plan' includes taking care of her health. She treats herself to a stay on a health farm, tries to eat sensibly and gives herself 'treats' such as facials and hair-dos. She is very keen on bridge and says that if you learn to play you can be sure that you will have friends for life. 'You need never be lonely.'

Katherine's insurance was planned ahead. She said she had read letters from unmarried daughters who had given up everything to devote themselves to their parents and had no resources after they had gone.

'Since my father's death, I've had a holiday and then, in June, I took up a part-time secretarial job. I kept up my friendships and interests so that they were there, waiting. And I am happy with my own company whenever I am alone.'

Phyllis Bush is a lady who has had her share of being left alone, though the grieving in her case was that of a deserted wife. She has been responsible for setting up singles clubs and lonely hearts agencies with a great deal of success and says that bereavement presents the same problems. When the shock has worn off, and the sympathetic friends have settled back in to their own family routines, you realize you are very much alone.

She is often asked for advice on emotional and practical issues such as love and friendship, decision-making and marriage. 'The first step is not to sit at home, feeling sorry for yourself,' she stressed. 'Get out and start to make contact with new acquaintances on your own terms. You feel lonely, yes, but you also have a new freedom, so use it. Assert your personal tastes and values. Redecorate the house, take your own decisions. Without someone else to consult, it can be overwhelming, at first, but after a while, confidence and self-respect will start to grow.'

Phyllis also advises that you should not rate your abilities and potential so low that you feel everyone else must be brighter than yourself. A woman left on her own is emotionally vulnerable, especially if she is a caring person. Suddenly, there is this emptiness, and in her search for something or someone to fill it, she may be deceived. I spoke to one carer who, within a year of the death of her parent, had fallen quite heavily for two men, both with the capacity to hurt her. The pattern in both cases had been similar: an unexpected meeting, interest shown on the part of the man and an invitation out. She had fallen for both of them and, for a while, gone about feeling 'happy and confident about life again'. For several reasons – neither man was suitable, and she expected too much of the relationships too soon – both had ended in disaster and she had been devastated, feeling far worse than before.

Far better, as Phyllis Bush suggests, to mix more generally, to go to as many group activities as possible and just become a member of the human race again, without great expectations. Psychologists are aware that the first relationship after a divorce or separation is fraught with pitfalls. Much the same might be said of those first faltering steps towards realizing self in a single ex-carer.

P.M. agreed. 'Be kind to yourself,' she said. 'Have that hair-do you have always wanted to try – the clothes you can just about afford. If you want to do something, do it. It won't take away the loneliness and the ache inside but it is a good rehabilitation step forward.'

There is support within the church, too, as Father D. said. 'It is a caring community, a way of getting back into society and making relationships with other people. If people do not make the first move there is nothing that can be done to help them.' He finds that some people try to treat him as a social worker and would be quite happy if he would just pop in, every week, for a cup of tea. 'There are situations when I know I must withdraw – the job of the parish priest is to lead the church community, but you cannot be relied on to counsel in all social situations.' His advice to the carer is to try to see what was enjoyed in the past and attempt to pick it up again; this is far preferable to sitting around at home.

Sometimes, according to Jenny Symons, people can seem a little too bold. She told the story of one woman who had discussed with her dying husband the need for her to remarry. He suffered from cancer for two years, during which time they grieved his dying together. When she saw Jenny, she said: 'I've got to get married again. I have gone through my grief while he was alive.' She advertised and answered advertisements, and within six months she had remarried. 'Maybe it was a defence against grieving,' said Jenny, 'rather like the man who tried to persuade himself that women were interchangeable, so that when his wife had died he tried to invite out his counsellor.'

In common with other carers, I try to put on a brave face and get on with life. But there are those days when you feel you would like to curl up in a small ball. You feel defeated – it just seems as if you cannot pick up the threads, it's all too late and you wonder whether it was all worthwhile. I have been impressed by some carers' courage. Dorothy does not agree with her son's 'perfect solution' of buying a house together so that she can have a granny flat. 'I said to them "I love you both dearly but I wouldn't want my daughter-in-law to go through what I have done. I'll come to you for holidays but keep my independence."' P.M. is philosophical, resigned to the fact that there will be no one when she may need care. She has her 'little bottle of tablets'. 'If there is a holocaust, if life becomes unbearable, I think everyone has the right to choose. I don't believe in just keeping people going.'

But perhaps, in the end, that is what all of us do: keep going, whether we are cared for or caring, and it is sometimes a very uneven track. One thing I found very encouraging was that even if the 'old-fashioned' carers may be becoming a little thin on the ground, there is a growing body of voluntary and professional people who do seem to care. They are like the wonderful people from Cruse who will stay until the bereaved feel strong enough to carry on with life on their own again. And even then it is not a final goodbye, as Jenny Symons pointed out: everyone she has counselled has her phone number and knows that Jenny will always be interested to hear what she has made of her new life.

8. The Future

When I began to write this book, my own days of caring were scarcely over, and I was floundering, confronted by my sense of loss and by the seemingly impossible task of coming to terms with bereavement and picking up the pieces. In my isolation, throughout that time when I often felt I was separated by a wall of glass from the outside world, where everybody seemed to be going about their lives, free of care, I had not really registered that there was an invisible army of people who, like me, were fighting the same lonely battle. I was bound up in my own situation, in my personal problems, which had gradually overtaken me, and I had tried to deal with them in the unsatisfactory way of muddling through. It seldom crossed my mind that caring could become an organized campaign of action with the back-up of outside facilities, nor had I considered the possibility of pooling ideas and experiences with other carers. All these options have presented themselves in the course of writing this book. I was, if you like, a novice carer, but then so are the majority of other carers, or at least of those I have spoken to. There is usually no rehearsal, no one to counsel you on how it should be done. You cope, or you don't, and, inevitably, there are times when you feel you have failed.

Anyone who takes on the carer's role usually does it by choice, and because you are seen by the 'outside world' to have chosen to do it, you are sometimes criticized for being 'weak', for not having enough backbone to leave it to 'them': those amorphous authorities. If you smile a little wryly to yourself because you know the reality of the situation, you are to be excused; it is still the case in Britain today that if you are a carer and are seen to be coping with the situation you are unlikely to receive much in the way of outside help. That's not just my opinion but one borne out by research carried out by the Equal Opportunities Commission.

After my mother died, and as I began to research this book, I started on a journey that would take me into the worlds of many carers, both formal and informal, and as I met them, I realized that I had never been alone, however lonely I had felt. Our society teems with carers, and the problem is increasing. And talking to these carers, or reading their letters, I have felt saddened by the burden many of these people bear. For the most part they feel isolated, frustrated, angry and despairing, but soldier on with the 'brave face' which hides the true extent of their needs. I have also been intimidated by the pessimism of those who see in the rising rate of divorce, the dispersal of families and general changes in our social structure, a blank future for all of us who, when the moment comes, may need care. On the other hand, I have been considerably heartened by the many splendid people who are making it possible for those who become less capable to stay where they usually want to be – in their own homes, among their own things.

This outward journey has been paralleled by an interior odyssey. It began with my departure from all that was known and familiar to me, and had been for as long as I can remember, in an endeavour to discover a new haven. And as I come to the end of this book I feel that I am a different person to the one who began it. I have not yet found that haven, I am still in transit, and possibly I share this feeling with some of the single women carers I have met since. But I know there are those who do find it, and I turn again to P.M., who seems to have accomplished the rite of passage with real success.

I believe I have now come to terms with the fact that it may take a considerable period of my life fully to understand and accept my loss, although I am already less diminished. I have been lucky in having the support of some wonderful people who have rallied round – sometimes to do no more nor less than listen. I can now laugh with my sister when we share happy, bygone memories; and I have felt a glow over small satisfactions. I have met several nice people and deepened my relationship with others, seen new places that I like and revisited familiar ones with fresh eyes. Activities begin to absorb me again and I plan new projects. If I am honest with myself, my life has not, as I imagined at one time, come to an end, and although it will never be quite the same again, I know I will survive. But I have lost someone who is irreplaceable.

I have also come to realize that there are traps into which it is easy for anyone in my position to fall. I agree with Tony Lake when he writes of the need to 'be' with integrity. Somehow, he says, we must resist developing into either a parasite or a hermit when we have been cut loose from a situation and are floating in the limbo which follows. For if we become too dependent, either on a set of circumstances or on someone else, we lose a part of that integrity. We become 'a mere colony of that person instead of a country in our own right'. If we fly for shelter under someone else's defences we will never make the effort to build up our own, and such a loss of completeness can never be compensated for by the small sense of purpose we gain.

But we have to strike a balance, says Dr Lake, for if we go to the other extreme and isolate ourselves completely from other people we cannot expect to achieve completeness, either. 'Somewhere between the two extremes we can be ourselves, asking for and giving help, knowing why we live and being nobody else but ourselves.'

I have learned some valuable lessons on the nature of grieving from Tony Lake and Jenny Symons. I understand now that it is no use trying to find something or someone who will 'rescue' you, because you only end up either being more dependent than ever before, or isolated and unloved. Grief throws these demands into the spotlight and forces us to face up to duties we have avoided. That is hard. But I know that now I am launched on this path I cannot go back; I have to try to find that balance between my twin tendencies to lean on someone or something and to isolate myself, if I want to move forward and find a fulfilled life.

When I broached the subject of 'picking up the pieces', Edna Smith took a somewhat bleak view. Certainly, she agreed, it would be nice to think that every carer could do so, that we could have 'a nicely rounded off story of caring' but, she added, 'life isn't like that'. The personal destiny of a carer, after the person she has cared for has died is not something that is possible to generalize about, she said. It depends on the relationship, the age at which the carer was 'freed'.

For a widow or widower, it can mean devastating loneliness or release from a huge burden, depending on the closeness of the relationship. But for the majority of carers, the prospect of being cared for themselves when the moment arrives is usually very slender indeed. Very few carers would want to put such a strain on someone else, especially someone they care for. Rather than impose such a burden, Edna Smith believes that most would hope to 'manage somehow'.

But 'managing' often boils down to a question of money. As I write this, I recall how many carers wrote to me of financial worries, and I wonder how they are coping. There is Joyce who must now be coming to the end of her and her mother's savings, wondering what she will do next; Caroline who is paying a retinue of four women on a rota basis, so that she can continue to work; and Jean who is recovering from her nervous breakdown, brought on because she and her husband just could not afford a week or two of respite for themselves and their severely handicapped charge.

Paul Endersby has been seconded from social services to coordinate the East Sussex involvement in a three-year community care scheme. He foresees an impending crisis as these and many many more carers reach breaking point. 'The problem is here and it has to be solved,' he said. 'Because families are no longer nuclear and mothers are often working, there is another problem which has got to be recognized: the employment situation. If there is a dependant in the family or home, it is going to affect a whole range of other areas, raise all sorts of different problems, and if this isn't realized there will be a crisis. There are many women who are faced with the problem of whether to work or stay at home; whether to pay someone else so that they can at least get out sometimes. They want to care for their dependants; they don't want to hand it over to someone else.'

But, as Paul Endersby and many other people in the caring professions predict, there will be fewer female carers in the next forty years who either can or are willing to stay at home to look after a dependant.

I can identify with the feelings of many carers who suffer financial anxieties over extra heating, special food and clothing, transport, laundry and possibly incontinence aids. According to a recent estimate, a family needs £2,500 extra per year, to care for an elderly dependant. My mother reached the stage where she could no longer walk and I regret that she did not have one of the streamlined wheelchairs that I saw bowling up and down the promenades of the Costa Geriatrica. Eventually, I managed to track down a source – our local Red Cross association. It is a marvellous organization which does excellent work but, obviously, there is not a great deal of choice: one takes what is going. Ours was a rickety old contraption and she was afraid she would be tilted out of it, so that idea was not very successful. But I should add that, in common with many other carers, I was not aware of other avenues I might have explored to obtain a better chair.

Guidelines are very important, even those which might seem obvious. Age Concern has recently produced some from its storehouse of information. It was worried because 35 per cent of pensioners entitled to the supplementary benefit did not claim. When winter threatens with heavy fuel bills, the elderly may take risks themselves in order to keep them down. The benefit system is becoming increasingly complex because of financial changes, which may be one reason why many people do not claim. A booklet for pensioners called *Your Rights*, and available from Age Concern, sets out every entitlement and incorporates all the latest changes. Carers would also be interested to know that the National and Provincial Building Society have entered the home income plan field and offer interest repayment mortgages to enable older borrowers to buy annuities to increase their income.

I was impressed recently by the frank article in *Today* by journalist Jane Adams, commenting on the 'forgotten army' of carers. It echoed my feelings about the battle which carers have to wage. As she commented, there are so many strings attached to the existing state allowances that the vast majority of carers are left out in the cold: 'Now they are looking to Europe for help to overcome government meanness as the numbers of Britain's elderly continue to grow rapidly.' The favourable decision in the European Court of Justice allowing married women to claim the Invalid Care Allowance could benefit more than 78,000 carers immediately, at a cost of £80 million a year. According to Jane Adams, however, this payment only scratches the surface.

The ever-increasing number of elderly people has presented a major challenge, which the Government has at last been pressurized to meet. A 'Care for the Carers' scheme, which is part of the DHSS programme 'Helping the Community to Care', has just been launched, at the time of writing. At long last there does seem to be some formal recognition of the huge invisible band of carers. Describing the background to this project, Paul Endersby said that, up until now, support services, both statutory and voluntary, have been extremely limited and even where they are available, carers are frequently unaware of their existence. In addition, carers often find support from each other, and the establishment and servicing of carers' groups, providing them with both information and emotional support, can assist in alleviating some of the stresses.

Three areas in Britain have been selected as demonstration zones and these contrast quite sharply with one another. The smallest is Stockport with a population of 250,000, then there is Sandwell in the Midlands with 350,000 and the largest, East Sussex, with 650,000.

'Care for the Carers' will aim to develop initiatives to support informal carers and, more specifically, to help families, voluntary organizations and others who care for dependent people in their own homes. A considerable amount of money is being put into it by the government, £200,000 per annum for three years, and it is administered by a consortium of voluntary organizations, with health and social services as full members. Grants will be made by the consortium, based on applications from voluntary organizations and groups.

'We might, for example, have half a dozen applications from groups to provide sitting services for the elderly,' said Paul Endersby, 'but we must make sure that we reflect the range of needs across the country. We want to look at ideas that will present new angles, at new projects that will teach us new lessons. For this we need to take a very individual approach. The informal carer is in the best position to know what is needed, for she – or he – is with the dependant all the time. Both their needs and the way in which they would like them to be met will vary. To give an example, not all carers want to be part of a carers' group, but at the same time, they need help: often practical, sometimes emotional. Again, it does not follow that all carers, however desperate their situation, want to receive "just a sitting service" to enable them to get out and about. They may prefer an alternative – to have their dependant cared for elsewhere, or respite care to enable them to relax in their own homes.'

With an elderly widowed mother himself, Paul Endersby is no jaundiced social services officer. He can identify with the conflicts of the carers he meets, and he has entered on this project with enthusiasm, hopeful that it will open the eyes of many professionals to the extent of carers' problems and what they need – how to have access to these services.

'It's no use leaving it up to the primary health services,' he said. 'Often, they don't know either.'

I can corroborate that!

One of the currently fashionable words in the social services is 'package'. The idea behind a carer package would be that of sending in a group of different people with different skills who would provide for the varying requirements of the dependant. The health visitor would initiate this, going into the home to assess the situation and then drawing on a range of options, which might be computerized for easy access to information.

As we spoke, Paul Endersby and I were reminded of a moment in that video film, *Time to be Me*, when a group of 'professionals' was pictured, representing the sheer number required to relieve all the varying tasks of the carer: there were fifteen in all. They could not have created a more telling image of the time and energy required in this little-recognized labour of love, caring for a dependant.

I could not help wondering if this three-year scheme will be able to achieve any lasting respite for those who care – or whether it will be just a flash in the pan and, at the end of the day, the burden will be laid back, fairly and squarely, at the carers' doors. I hope that I am wrong to doubt its success.

It is very difficult to scribble out a prescription to satisfy all carers' needs, as Paul Endersby acknowledged, but there are some general needs which are common to everyone. Meeting these would help to make the lives of those old people within the community, and their carers, more comfortable. Edna Smith outlined them for me.

She sees the need for good communication lines which are 'sure, speedy and safeguarded against misuse by miscreants'. These should be linked to emergency services in case of crisis – police, doctor, fire brigade, gas, electricity, plumbing, etc. All this should be operated via one central control which could be permanently manned by responsible people.

Positive steps toward ensuring this kind of reliable communication service to as many of Britain's elderly as possible have recently been taken by several district councils;

one example is the community alarm scheme implemented by Adur district council, in West Sussex. It uses an advanced model of telephone which, in times of trouble, provides an emergency link with a control centre. It can be the constant companion of an elderly person, 'caring' for him or her twenty-four hours a day, all the year round, and not only that, it could save his life. The alarm operates by activating a neck pendant trigger or, alternatively, by pressing an emergency button on the phone which will connect the caller with a professionally trained control centre staff. Immediate help can thus be summoned, and there are also sensors within the unit which can be programmed to warn of hypothermia, fire or burglary. A major appeal has been launched by Help the Aged with the aim of raising £16 million during the next two years in order to provide most of Britain's old people with such units. This forms a major part of the charity's silver jubilee programme. Help the Aged has selected the 'Lifeline' model because it has a remote answering facility, of particular use to the disabled, bedridden or people slow on their feet.

Those who are temporarily or permanently housebound, said Edna Smith, need someone they can talk to. Authorities are hopeful that the installation of an alarm system which could involve the neighbours as standby may become a springboard for greater personal involvement. Technology is all very well but the human touch is equally if not more valuable to those who cannot go out.

The impressive medical and social services of Denmark, which Edna Smith studied during her visits there, have convinced her it would do nothing but good to improve our own in Britain. She would like to see mobile nurses of both sexes available to visit an elderly person who is not feeling well at home, on a daily basis or even more frequently, and thus be able to assess when it was time to call a doctor. Another suggestion was a local, small, short-term sick bay attached to a residential home for those in need of more continual nursing for a few days but not the resources of a hospital.

She also pointed out that many elderly people would appreciate help in finding reliable and trustworthy people to do any work necessary at a reasonable cost, such as those teams of retired craftsmen who have set themselves up in various parts of the country to help older people. And there should be encouragement of neighbourhood watch groups, to deter criminal activities. 'Older people can be very effective "look outs", even from indoors,' she said.

It is probable that we could persuade friends and neighbours to help us out, to keep an eye on elderly people and offer a little tea and sympathy. But what if there is someone from an ethnic minority living in your street? Are most people inclined, as writer Allison Norman has suggested, to distinguish between 'our' elderly and 'their' elderly; and do we continue to believe that 'they' look after their own?

This is a problem that will increasingly confront us in Britain, as time goes by: that of the specific needs of elderly people from ethnic minorities who form part of our mixed society. Charities such as Age Concern have already recognized this. They set up a course which attempted to identify these needs and how services might be provided to meet them. During a day conference, Allison Norman, who wrote *Triple Jeopardy*, painted a pessimistic picture of life for the ethnic minority. The three 'jeopardies' of her book are: age, colour and lack of access to benefits and facilities.

There is need for special services, she says, but meeting this need is a complex and difficult task. Some of the responsibility must rest with the minority communities for not pressing for appropriate services. They are doing a lot themselves but their voluntary efforts ought to be supported by statutory services.

The problem is also being looked into by Geoffrey Ward, Ethnics Minorities Inspector for Birmingham social services. His task is to re-orientate services so that they have a multi-cultural approach. The various services are examined to check whether they are relevant and acceptable and to look at what the alternatives might be. Then an effort is made to recruit and train staff from ethnic minorities and to retrain existing staff where necessary. The services must also take into account the differences within each ethnic group, so that there is no stereotyping. While Geoffrey Ward acknowledges that the community groups can be helpful, this does not mean the local authority can opt out. Overall, he feels that people should not accept services 'as they come', but should badger the providers to meet their special needs in the way they feel they should be met. It is a suggestion that could usefully be followed by all the elderly of this country!

Another trend which will surely affect the future of both cared for and carers, now and as they grow older, is that of earlier retirement. This is something that has been developing in the United States for some time, and it is now becoming increasingly normal in Britain for people of fifty-five plus, even forty-five plus, to find themselves faced by retirement before they have had time really to contemplate it. Bill Bruce, who is director of the Pre-retirement Association, feels that we should examine closely what we can do to help in this area. Retirement today has a completely different meaning from that of twenty years ago. It can mean an unused resource of human capital which should be re-invested, for the sake of both the individual and the community in which he lives. This has always been the case but now, with dramatically earlier ages of retirement, it is even more important to use the talent and experience that would otherwise go to waste.

'We have to get down to the task of considering new forms of early planning, to meet the needs of those who, increasingly, find their full-time working careers terminated well in advance of what is considered the orthodox age for retirement.'

Bill Bruce is planning other developments, such as a closer liaison with regional and local organizations. There is a continually expanding network of pre-retirement bodies, all run on a voluntary basis, with the occasional part-time administrator or organizer.

His hope is for greater coordination and communication with other organizations. 'In catering for the needs of older people there must be overlaps between organizations, and I wonder if we as an Association can become involved in the post-retirement area. Some of our most successful local groups have done this to their credit.' But as Bill Bruce is at pains to point out, whatever edifices are raised in retirement planning, at base they must all rest on that phrase 'the human situation'.

This is certainly a *leitmotif* in that excellent publication, *Choice*, one of the comparatively recent collection of magazines catering for the over-fifties and one which I have enjoyed reading. It reflects a group in our society with rights and attitudes of its own – health, finance and property are admirably covered, and features include readers' accounts of how there certainly is life after retirement. And it would seem, that *Choice* readers are not generally the 'retiring type' any more than our most illustrious pensioner, Her Majesty Queen Elizabeth, who is featured in a recent issue. It does seem a pity that the magazines which cater for younger readers often persist in stereotyping age.

It was *Choice* magazine in association with the Park Hill Trust which founded the scheme called 'New Horizons'. Groups have been encouraged to dream up imaginative and worthwhile undertakings which will be of benefit to their localities and will also encourage those who are past retirement age to reinvest their skills and brains. Should the proposals be selected by 'New Horizons', the group is awarded up to £5,000 to get launched. The 'New Horizons' booklet, A First Report serves to underline the variety of projects which have been assisted. In Cheltenham, over £2,000 has gone to a group of retired craftsmen who now pass on their skills to the unemployed, to the physically handicapped and to pensioners. Another grant of over £4,000 was made to a group in Shipley who are producing a talking newspaper for the blind. The members, who aim to triple their audience, read, record and edit news from the local newspaper onto a master tape and this grant is meeting the cost of the equipment.

Typical of the projects described in the booklet was the

effort of a handful of over-sixties in Wellingborough to form a brass band. Members included retired Salvation Army bandsmen who were keen not only to continue playing but also to teach new members. A further cash award has gone into research on computers to help the blind.

Gloomy predictions of the supply and demand ratio of homes for retired people seem, unfortunately, as if they will be fulfilled. It is almost impossible to keep pace with the growing need. According to one company, Bellway Retirement Homes, the total requirement for retired people, working on the premise that 17 per cent of the population is of pensionable age, is an estimated 250,000 to 400,000 units. But, it points out, new accommodation for only 15,000 such people is provided every year. And that imbalance can only increase as time goes by. Bellway underline that retirement homes fulfill the need to provide comfortable, easily maintained houses for elderly people. They are ideal for those who are still fit enough to lead busy and active lives but who appreciate having a warden on call, in case of illness or accidents. The friendly atmosphere of a retirement home, and the ever-ready help, suggests that it will be one of the most highly preferred solutions in the future.

Martens Court is a typical retirement home which follows the trends of this future development for the elderly. It was built by Wimpey, who have moved into this expanding sector of the market. The area is excellently served by buses to almost anywhere, it seems; there is a nearby railway station and even an accessible airport. The amenities, which are ideal for the elderly person, include a nearby indoor shopping precinct where one can browse in warmth and comfort. There are two group medical practices, dental facilities, opticians and orthopaedic facilities. The neighbouring Martens Grove park has a lovely open stretch of matured garden and there is every kind of sporting and entertainment activity in the vicinity. The development would seem to supply Edna Smith's 'prescription' for the elderly, although she does not like the idea of such segregation by age. But if the fun-packed and jolly lives of those who live in the American development Sun City are anything to go by, even segregation might have much in its favour. Situated in Utah, Arizona, this is the ultimate in catering for the old: it seems the days cannot be long enough for the range of activities it offers.

Home owners over the age of sixty-five who are finding it difficult to make ends meet have been offered another appealing plan. This is new and seems set for a successful future. It is called the Home Reversal Plan, whereby elderly people can sell their existing homes and purchase one, a new, converted one- or two-bedroom flat, currently priced from £17,600. The flat then remains in the buyer's ownership for the rest of his or her life, rent and interest free. The only other liability other than the usual outgoings is a maintenance charge of approximately £120 a year. This scheme is appropriate for elderly people living on low incomes and unable to unlock the capital value contained in their property. Further details may be obtained from Haley Partners (see Appendix 2).

For those in need of more intensive care, the Anchor Housing Trust expects to start building its first housing scheme for frail old people in the near future. This will provide flats for thirty-one people, meals will be available and there will be round-the-clock staffing and help available to every resident, in dealing with day-to-day routines. The Trust is also hoping to buy a site in a village on the outskirts of Plymouth. This would provide lovely housing for the elderly and frail, with the same support and care which is offered in the other developments. It hopes in the future to be able to provide further housing for such needy older people.

At the risk of repeating myself, but because it is so vital to stress it, I believe that the best insurance we can give ourselves is to make a positive attempt to build and maintain our health. This applies equally to carers and those they care for. It is, therefore, encouraging to see the increasing amount of attention which is being paid to health and fitness for the older person and I welcome it, in particular as it goes a long way towards destroying the stereotype of old age. Not everyone becomes decrepit and bent double the instant they pass their fiftieth birthday.

Olive Double was forty-five before she took up swimming seriously and went in for her teaching certificates. She is particularly proud of her sports personality award from the Epping Forest District Council, given for her 'outstanding achievement with the fifties and over'. Olive believes that television has had the positive effect of making everyone more sports conscious. 'People see swimmers and gymnasts on the screen and it encourages them to have a go.' Her future plans include taking yoga to those who are disabled. 'There are lots of helpful things they can be taught – I don't mean standing on the head or anything like that. But it really is necessary to exercise as much as possible even if you are chairbound.'

Olive illustrates a sector of this increasing span of interest, which takes in the provision and use of leisure facilities for and by elderly people, and new work on the physical capabilities of older people, their increasing involvement in sport, the effect of exercise on general health and mobility, and the connection between physical, mental and emotional health. But we should not stop there; health includes watching what we eat, too.

Britain still lags behind other countries' health programmes designed to cut down one of the modern killers, heart disease. Unlike other Western countries, our extremely high rate has changed very little in the past ten years. But we could reduce the incidence of heart attacks and strokes by 30 per cent by the year 2,000, according to Dr John Catford, who is employed by the Wessex Health Authority. He has started a scheme whereby funds will be allocated to those organizations and activities whose aim is to involve the inactive minority in healthy recreations. Age Concern, whose involvement in so many aspects of caring is a reflection of the dedication of the people concerned, is also interested in leisure activities for older people. It organized a seminar, which included representatives from the Sports Council, to develop a programme of regional activities which could lead to national events. More and more, people are recognizing that we must put emphasis on preventative medicine if we are not going to strain the health service far beyond its endurance. I was, for example, impressed by the idea of Healthline, an experimental initiative from the College of Health. Anyone living in London, Exeter or Gloucester can pick up the phone and ask for one of the hundred or more tapes on a wide range of health topics. All information has been checked and approved by a medical committee and will be updated continually. Each tape gives a brief outline of one medical condition, describes the symptoms and explains what treatment might be. It also suggests when a visit to the doctor might be advisable and gives tips on looking after your own health. I know, from my own experience, that it would certainly have been of great help to me as a carer.

Of course an important component of good health is a positive attitude: having an aim in life, according to Dr Keith Thompson, author of *Caring for an Elderly Relative*. I have been pleasantly surprised by the number of older people who are making plans for the future; those, for example, who make the most of the extended holiday offers of several tour operators in Britain. This has a double value: it gives people something to look forward to and also helps to keep them healthy.

'Getting the sun on your back, every winter' is comedian Ernie Wise's prescription, both as an aim of later years, and to build optimum health. He is, incredibly, a pensioner, who flies to where the sun and warmth are guaranteed, in Fort Lauderdale, Southern Florida. There, a 'whole fairyland' opens up to him. 'One vast playground just waiting to be enjoyed and in particular by senior citizens.' There he owns an apartment and within the complex of which it forms part there is a club house, indoor and outdoor swimming pools, tennis courts . . . and security, 'which is so important, these days'.

Writing in *Choice*, he said, 'The Americans really work hard at retirement. They go out jogging, cycling and swimming, play lots of tennis and generally indulge in all kinds of physical exercise. Their enthusiasm is frightening and infectious and you find yourself wishing everyone a nice day and meaning it. You never see mature people sitting about and moping. To them, life is a banquet, and it is hard not to be active and in good cheer there, given the warmth and seemingly endless sunshine.'

As Ernie Wise admits, not everybody can afford to buy their own place in the sun but there are some most reasonable all-in holiday deals in the brochures. Many companies seem to be bending over backwards to cater for the older traveller who, perhaps for the first time in his life, has the opportunity to go away without a thought for anyone else. One resort, Benidorm on the Spanish Costa Blanca, has always had the reputation of being something of a kiss-me-quick destination. This might be so in summer, but in the off-peak season, it is completely different. Many elderly people have taken to going there, year in, year out, and the town is now planning a much more upmarket image. Plans are going ahead for three new hotels with a five star rating and life will be more peaceful when traffic on the Levante beach road is restricted to emergency vehicles only. The town will be gentler, prettier, with flower-filled stone urns, shrubs and small trees, and there will be tree-lined walkways, winding jogging tracks, a lake, picnic areas and cafeterias. The chances are that the elderly will take over.

I already knew of one or two companies which cater for 'third age' travellers, but was surprised by the sheaf of brochures I collected from my travel agent, resplendent with names like 'Young at Heart' 'Golden Days' and 'Golden Age' holidays. The offers are very tempting: 'Why not forget the soaring bills and bleak weather back in England?' they urge. 'Visit new places, meet new friends, discover new interests – all in the warm, relaxing comfort of a kinder climate.' It seems a very positive turn in the process of becoming older if such an Indian summer awaits one. The brochures also display a wealth of holidays of special interest to the elderly, featuring such activities as sequence dancing, bridge, whist and bowls.

'Perhaps for the first time in your life you have time to spare, the opportunity to enjoy a winter break in the sun', runs another brochure. It also suggests that it is cheaper and healthier for many older people to spend weeks, even months in Spain than to suffer our British winter. Another company, Yugotours, has looked to the older market as part of their plan to boost year-round holidays in Yugoslavia. Their 'Golden Age' holidays are described as 'an affordable alternative for those who seem to search in vain, each winter, for a combination of sunshine, sophistication and economy'.

The pioneer in this fast expanding field was Saga, whose magazine is now popular reading among these get-up-and-go pensioners. In its early days, holidays were offered in Britain, often on university campuses during the vacations; now its clients travel the world.

The photographs in these magazines and brochures show men and women whose waistlines may have thickened, whose hair has turned grey, but who are still upright, mature but not incapacitated, enjoying the autumn of their lives. This is the bright side of the picture, but there is another: that of just carrying on, getting older and getting by. And this will continue to be the dreary future for many, unless we change our attitudes toward the old, and give more thought to the care they should receive in the Britain of today, which seems to have forgotten the enormous debt we owe them.

Epilogue

Was I a good carer? I often ask myself, and other people, that question. In talking to others who are, or have been, in the same position, it is inevitable that you compare yourself with them. I loved my mother deeply. I wanted to be with her. On the other hand, I don't deny I had a strong urge to establish my own identity. I often felt frustrated and there were times when I rebelled. Although I am certain I did not measure up to some of the super-Marthas who made an art and a job out of being a carer, I comfort myself by thinking that I performed a useful role by just 'being there'. 'The important thing is to know that someone will be coming in,' my mother said. 'I can put up with sitting alone a lot of the time when I know there is someone in the next room.'

Throughout this book, I have tried to give a two-dimensional view, for the cared for and the caring have much in common: both may feel isolated and friendless. The world often shrinks to containing just the two of them.

Jill Pitkeathley, recently appointed director of the National Council for Carers and their Elderly Dependants, has wisely said: 'You don't have to do anything. The most important thing you can do is just sit there and listen. We tend to want to offer solutions and give practical advice, suggest alternatives. When you feel tempted to do those things, remember that nothing is as precious as your time and your complete attention given to another person, especially if that person is distressed.' The skill of listening is sometimes instinctive, she says, but more often it has to be learned. I would add that that applies equally to caring.

Love, compassion, duty – whatever the motive for becoming a carer, it is a task that, once taken on, has to be seen through to the end. Perhaps I was fortunate, but I did not come across one single carer who found it possible to turn her back on the person she was caring for, although, like myself, I met many who would have wished for much more outside support and information.

Whatever is said by the doomwatchers of our future – of a world without family life or lasting attachments – I remain optimistic about the human race. From what I have seen we still possess sentiment and other so-called old-fashioned feelings, and long may they survive. In a society which no longer cares for its young, old and defenceless, we will have truly arrived at barbarianism.

Which Benefit?

Which Benefit? is a free booklet (FB2) published by the DHSS, available at your local DHSS office; it covers all benefits and how to apply for them, and also tells you which leaflet to get to tell you more about them, for instance . . .

Looking After Someone at Home (NP27), available from the DHSS, and *Your Rights*, available from Age Concern.

Leaflets are also available from public libraries, Citizens' Advice Bureaux, some post offices, and from individual charities and pressure groups (addresses given in *Which Benefit?*).

Supplementary Benefit

A weekly cash payment to people aged 16 and over who are not working full-time and who do not have enough money to live on; a woman who gives up work to look after her elderly mother, for example. You can receive this on top of other benefits, or earnings from part-time work. If you are an owner occupier you can get help with your rates; if you are a tenant, help from the council with your rent and rates; if you are buying (or own) your home you may be able to get help with your mortgage interest, insurance and maintenance costs. You may also get lump sum payments for special needs. A typical payment is £29.80 a week for a single householder, plus the allowance for rent and rates.

Health Benefits

People getting supplementary benefit or housing benefit supplement also, automatically, get free NHS prescriptions, glasses, dental treatment and hospital travelling expenses.

There is also leaflet SB17, *Help with Heating Costs*, for people getting supplementary benefit.

Free Hospital Appliances
NHS out-patients and day patients who are on supplementary benefit or housing benefit supplement get free appliances. Even if you don't have an automatic right to them, you could get them free (or obtain some help with the cost) if you don't have much money coming in. If you want to know more, ask at the hospital.

Free NHS Hearing Aids
People of all ages with impaired hearing, for whom a hearing aid is prescribed by a consultant, can get NHS hearing aids on free loan. The aid will be supplied and fitted, serviced, maintained and supplied with batteries. If you want to know more, ask your doctor.

Hospital Travelling Expenses
You may be able to get travelling expenses to and from hospital paid if you are an in-patient or an out-patient. If you need someone to travel with you, their travelling expenses will be paid as well. This benefit is means-tested, except for some war pensioners and many people living in the Scottish Highlands and Islands or the Isles of Scilly.

Going into Hospital – effect on Benefits and Pensions
When you go into hospital, some of your needs that have been met by your benefits or pensions will be met instead by the National Health Service. While you are there, some of your benefits may be temporarily reduced or stopped.

Attendance Allowance

This is for people who need a lot of looking after because they are severely disabled, physically or mentally. It can be claimed on top of any other income and/or benefits you receive. The lower rate, for day *or* night attendance or supervision, is £20.65 a week; the higher rate, for day *and* night attendance or supervision, is £30.95 a week.

Invalid Care Allowance

This is for people of working age who give up work to look after someone who is receiving the attendance allowance. Until recently, a woman who was married or living as a married woman was not eligible for ICA. Then in June 1986 the European Court of Justice decided that the rule no longer applied. Now the ICA rate for all women is £23.25 a week.

Mobility Allowance

For those between five and 75 unable, or virtually unable, to walk; to help with the cost of getting about. You must qualify before the age of 65, claim before the age of 66. The weekly rate is £21.65.

Housing Benefit

You may be able to get help from your local council whether you are working or not, if you find it hard to pay your full rent or rates. If you are a council tenant, you can apply for a rent rebate; if a private tenant, a rent allowance. You can apply for a rates rebate whether you are a council or a private tenant, or an owner occupier. The amount of help you can get depends on how much money you have coming in and how much in rent and rates you have to pay.

Rate Relief for Disabled People

This is for people who are disabled and for whom special alterations or additions have had to be made to their homes because of their particular disability. Owner occupiers, council or private tenants, or members of their household can apply. For more information get leaflet *Rate Relief for Disabled Persons* from your local council offices, library or Citizens' Advice Bureau (in Scotland from your regional or island's council offices).

Other Help and Services

People who are handicapped or disabled may get special help with a variety of services. The social services department of your local authority may be able to provide help with local bus and train fares, special aids and home adaptations, home helps, holidays, residential accommodation, day centres, meals on wheels, laundry, special housing, provision of television and telephone, advice from a social worker. The amount of help and the types available will depend on local circumstances and the local authority's assessment of your individual needs. Get leaflet HB.1, *Help for Handicapped People*; or if north of the border, *Help for Handicapped People in Scotland*. British Rail has a leaflet on the railcard for disabled people, available from stations.

Road Tax Exemption

If you are unable or virtually unable to walk you may get road tax exemption – this also applies if you are too disabled to drive yourself, get attendance allowance and have a vehicle registered in your name. Get form MHS 564 from DSB7C (VEDE) DHSS, Block 1, Government Buildings, Warbreck Hill Road, Blackpool FY2 OUZ.

Retirement Pension

This is for men over 65 and women over 60 who have retired from work. If you don't retire at this age you can earn extra pension. After the age of 70 (men) and 65 (women) you get your pension no matter how much work you do.

Over 80 Pension

This is for people aged 80 or over who are entitled to a national insurance retirement pension of less than £23 a week, or none at all. Married women and widows whose husbands were born before 6 July 1883 also qualify for a non-contributory pension. Ask at your local social security office for more details.

Supplementary Pension

If your pensions don't give you enough to live on, you may be able to get supplementary pension on top of them. The rules and additional benefits are the same as for supplementary benefit.

Tax Allowances

If you want to know more about your tax position when you retire, get leaflet IR.4 from a tax office or PAYE enquiry office.

Legal Advice and Assistance

If you are living on a low income you should obtain legal advice free or at a low cost, and also help with legal costs. The leaflet *Legal Aid for Civil and Criminal Cases: Getting Legal Help* may be obtained from a court, police station, public library or Citizens' Advice Bureau.

Reduced Fares

You can buy British Rail Senior Citizens Railcards if you are 60 or over. These allow you to buy many tickets at reduced prices. There are also free or reduced price travel facilities offered by some local transport services. Ask British Rail, London Regional Transport, or your local bus service for more information.

Death Grant

A single payment usually made to the next-of-kin, executor, or person paying the funeral expenses. Payment depends on the age of the person who has died.

Supplementary Benefit Lump Sum Payments
If it is up to you to arrange the funeral of a relative or someone who lived with you, and you are entitled to supplementary benefit, you may get help with the cost. Get leaflet D.49 *What to do After a Death*.

Useful Addresses

Action in Retirement Centre,
Bishopwearmouth Parish Church,
High Street,
West Sunderland, SR1
Tel: Sunderland 654066

Age Concern,
Bernard Sunley House,
Pitcairn Road,
Mitcham,
Surrey
Tel: 01 640 5431

Age Exchange Theatre,
(Pam Schweitzer),
Blackheath Village,
London SE3
Tel: 01 318 9105

Alzheimer's Disease Society,
Bank Lodges,
Fulham Broadway,
London SW6 IEP
Tel: 01 381 3177

Anchor Housing Association and Anchor Housing Trust,
Central Office: Oxenford House,
13/15 Magdalen Street,
Oxford OX1 3BP
Tel: Oxford 722261

Association of Carers,
Medway Homes,
21 New Road,
Chatham,
Kent ME4 6QU
Tel: Rochester 813981

British Association for the Hard of Hearing,
7 Armstrong Road,
London W3
Tel: 01 743 1110

British Rheumatism and Arthritis Association,
6 Grosvenor Crescent,
London SW1
Tel: 01 235 0902

Care for the Carers,
(Paul Endersby, Project Coordinator),
143 High Street,
Lewes,
East Sussex
Tel: Lewes 476819

Councils for Voluntary Services,
Look in your telephone book for address and telephone
number of local offices

Counsel and Care for the Elderly,
131 Middlesex Street,
London E1
Tel: 01 621 1624

Chest, Heart and Stroke Association,
Tavistock House (North),
Tavistock Square,
London WC1H 9JE
Tel: 01 387 3012

Crossroad Care Attendant Scheme,
94 Coton Road,
Rugby,
Warwickshire
Tel: Rugby 73653

Family Hospitality,
(Mrs Wendy Saunders),
24 Windlesham Road,
Brighton,
Sussex
Tel: Brighton 204175

Fish Scheme, The
Organized through churches to help in many neighbour-
hoods. One does not have to be a church member to benefit

Grace,
PO Box 71,
Cobham,
Surrey ET11 2JR
Tel: Cobham 62928
This organization keeps details of private homes outside
London

Haley Partners,
Highfield House,
37 South Street,
Worthing,
Sussex

Healthline,
PO Box 499,
London E2 9PF
Tel: 01 980 4848

Help the Aged,
St James's Walk,
London EC1R OBE
Tel: 01 253 0253

Holiday Care Service,
2 Old Bank Chambers,
Station Road,
Horley,
Surrey RG6 9HW
Tel: 01 273 74535

Homoeopathy – Faculty of,
The Royal London Homoeopathic Hospital,
Great Ormond Street,
London WC1
Tel: 01 837 3091

Invalid Caring Allowance Steering Group,
12 Park Crescent,
London W1 EEQ
Contact this organization for more information on the issue
of married women claiming this allowance

Keep Fit Association,
16 Upper Woburn Place,
London WC1H OQG
Tel: 01 387 4349

Marie Curie Memorial Foundation,
124 Sloane Street, or
28 Belgrave Square,
London SW1
Tel: 01 235 3325

Mind,
22 Harley Street,
London W1N 2ED
Tel: 01 637 0741

Northern Office:
155/157 Woodhouse Lane,
Leeds LS2 3EF
Tel: 0532 23926

Welsh Office:
7 St Mary Street,
Cardiff CF1 2AT
Tel: Cardiff 395123

National Council for Carers and their Elderly Dependants,
29 Chilworth Mews,
London W2 3RG
Tel: 01 724 7776

National Listening Library,
now merged with the British Library of Tape Recordings
for Hospital Patients (BLOT),
12 Lant Street,
Borough,
London SE1
Tel: 01 407 9417

National Society for Cancer Relief,
Anchor House,
15 Britten Street,
London SW3
Tel: 01 351 7811

New Horizons,
Choice Publications,
12 Bedford Row,
London WC1R 4DU
Tel: 01 404 4320

This is an organization run by *Choice* magazine with the Park Hill Trust to help pensioners who want to do something for their local communities

Parkinson's Disease Society,
36 Portland Place,
London W1
Tel: 01 323 1174

Saga Holidays,
PO Box 64
Folkestone,
Kent
Tel: 0303 30030

St John's Ambulance,
Check in your telephone book for local branch

Samaritans,
Check in your telephone book for local contact

Scottish Information Centre for the Disabled,
18 Claremont Crescent,
Edinburgh EH7 3QD
Tel: Edinburgh 556 3882

Shape,
9 Fitzroy Square,
London W1 6AE
This organization is concerned to make the arts physically and psychologically accessible to people with disabilities and special needs

University of the Third Age,
8a Castle Street,
Cambridge
Tel: Cambridge 321587

Voluntary Euthanasia Society,
13 Prince of Wales Terrace,
London W8 5PG
Tel: 01 937 7770

Wales Council for the Disabled,
Crescent Road,
Caerphilly,
Mid Glamorgan CF81 1X1
Tel: 022 869 224

Wimpey Homes Holdings Limited,
27 Hammersmith Grove,
London W6 7EN
Tel: 01 846 2610

WRVS Luncheon Clubs,
Ask at your Citizens' Advice Bureau for their local address

Further Reading

The 36-Hour Day – Caring at Home for Confused Elderly People
Learning to Care for Elderly People
The Older Patient
Your Rights
All published by Age Concern with Hodder and Stoughton, and available from Age Concern

Images of Ourselves – Disabled Women Talking
Help at Hand – a Signpost Guide for Carers
Caring: Experiences of Looking after Disabled Relatives
All published by Routledge and Kegan Paul, and available from the Association of Carers

Bassey, E. J. and Fentem, P. H., *Exercise – The Facts*, Oxford University Press, 1981

Briggs, Anna and Oliver, Judith, *Caring*, Routledge and Kegan Paul, 1985

British Telecom, *Guide to Equipment and Services for Disabled Customers*; available from local BT sales offices

Centre for Policy on Ageing: many leaflets on ageing, and learning facilities for the elderly. Available from their office at Nuffield Lodge, Regent's Park, London NW1 4RS (tel: 01 586 9844 for an appointment)

Chest, Heart and Stroke Foundation: *My Brother's Keeper*. This and many other useful books and leaflets available from the Foundation's offices at Tavistock House (North), Tavistock Square, London WC1H 9JE

Comfort, Alex, *A Good Age*, Mitchell Beazley, 1977

Conti, N., Davison, W. and Webster, S., *Age – The Facts*, Oxford University Press, 1984

Darby, Christine, *Keeping Fit While Caring*, Family Welfare Association, 1984; available from the Association of Carers

Denham, M. H. (ed.), *Care of the Long Stay Elderly Patient*, Croom Helm, 1983

Eves, Edward V., *Money and Your Retirement*; available from the Pre-Retirement Association, 19 Undine Street, London SW17 8PP

Fisher, Richard B., *A Dictionary of Mental Health*, Granada, 1980

Fulder, Stephen, *About Ginseng*, Thorsons, 1976

Fulder, Stephen, *An End to Ageing?*, Thorsons, 1983

Gibson, Joan, *Open the Window* (practical ideas for the lonely and depressed); may be ordered from Gateway Books, 19 Circus Place, Bath, Avon BA1 2PW

Gore, Irene, *Age and Vitality: Commonsense Ways of Adding Life to Your Years*, Allen and Unwin, 1979

Gray, Muir and McKenzie, Heather, *Take Care of Your Elderly Relative*, Allen and Unwin, 1980

Look After Yourself
The Time of Your Life: A Handbook for Retirement; available from the Health Education Council

Hudson, Peter, *Why Die Young?*, Pryor Publications, 1983

Hinewood, Melanie and Wicks, Malcolm, *The Forgotten Army: Family Care and Elderly People*, The Family Policy Studies Centre, 1984

Lake, Tony, *Living With Grief*, Sheldon Press, 1984

Lashak, David, *The Daily Telegraph Guide to Retirement*, Collins, 1978

Mandelstam, Dorothy, *Incontinence*; available from the Disabled Living Foundation

Nuffield Orthopaedic Centre, *Home Management* and *Housing and Furniture*, two books in the series 'Equipment for the Disabled'. (They contain details on a wide range of aids for use around the home, with notes on solutions for specific problems.) Available from the Nuffield Centre at Mary Marlborough Lodge, Headington, Oxford OX3 7LD

McKenzie, Heather, *If Only You Care*, SPCK, 1980

Moore, Sheila, *Working for Free: the Essential Handbook of Voluntary Work*, Severn House, 1977

Norman, Alison, *Triple Jeopardy*, Bailey Bros

Parker, R. Lucas, *Nature's Medicines*, New York, 1966

Sheehy, Gail, *Passages*, Dutton, New York, 1976

Stoppard, Miriam, *Fifty Plus Life Guide*, Dorling Kindersley, 1983

Thompson, Keith, *Caring for an Elderly Relative*, M. Dunitz, 1986

Whitaker, Agnes (ed.), *All in the End is Harvest – An Anthology for Those Who Grieve*, Darton, Longman and Todd, 1984

Wright, H. Beric, *In the Pink* (a *Choice* Magazine guide to good health in retirement); details from *Choice* Magazine, 12 Bedford Row, London WC1 4DU